TRAVELS *with* BILL

TRAVELS
with BILL

MARIETTA PRITCHARD

NORTHAMPTON, MASSACHUSETTS

Travels with Bill is published by
The Impress Group
Northampton, Massachusetts
Book designed by James McDonald
JAMESMCDONALDBOOKS.COM

ISBN 978-1-5323-7477-7
PRINTED IN THE UNITED STATES

Think only of the past as
its remembrance gives you pleasure.

—Mr. Darcy, *Pride and Prejudice*

Elizabeth Bennet

CONTENTS

TRAVELS
with BILL

Sometime in the late 1970s. Bill and I are standing in front of his aunts' house, two doors down from his childhood home in Johnson City, New York. We went there with our children every summer for many years.

He Said, She Said

W E DON'T TRAVEL as a couple anymore, Bill and I, except for the shortest jaunts to Boston maybe once a year, in the summer for a few days to the Adirondacks to visit Bill's brother and family, to the Berkshires where friends sometimes take us to indoor concerts at Tanglewood (Bill doesn't listen to music outdoors). So I travel on my own, but more and more rarely: day trips with a friend, twice-yearly trips to Oregon to keep in touch with son Will and family, once a year or so to the Washington, D.C., area to see my sister, rare overnights to New York. I also dig in more closely here at home—not as closely as Bill does with his piles of books and constant reviewing and teaching at Amherst College, but still, closely.

I walk, usually with the dog, and enjoy the local scene, one that changes with every quirk in the weather, time of day, seasonal decoration, home improvement, and new retail shop. I make small alterations in the routes we take— one day more sidewalk, another day more woods, more

open fields. The dog has become unreliable about returning to me when called, so I keep her closer, on leash most
of the time. We have worked with a trainer on her "recall,"
but I am wary of setting her free after two escapes under
irresistible fences. I find pleasure in my regular routine,
which varies enough to keep me grounded. I'm not as restless as I once was, it seems, not so much yearning to travel
or take part in more cultural activities, not so much yearning of any sort. Unlike the dog, I no longer ache to break
through fences. My daily round seems to be enough. That
includes reading—mostly novels and newspapers—along
with, until recently, writing my monthly columns for the
local paper, where I was once an editor, often working on
a longer writing project, volunteering at the local hospice,
playing tennis, going to yoga, and spending time with a
refugee from Nepal who wants to improve her spoken
English. These are the fixed points in my week. They
anchor me pretty well, and it's not too hard to improvise
around them. My mornings are mostly for writing, and
when I am in a good rhythm, I do five hundred words a day.
I cook an evening meal almost every night, do the laundry,
care for the garden, watch the finances, see that the house-
hold is kept up physically. We entertain less than in years
past. Partly there is less energy for this, and partly old friends

have vanished and younger ones seem less likely to want to share meals or drinks. We feed our local relatives—our eldest son, David's, family—as well as housing friends and relations who come to visit. It feels like a good life.

Recently, in an effort to get straight about our mutual and separate timelines ("What was the year we stayed in that funny inn in Cromer on the North Sea?"), Bill handed me the typed journals he's kept of some of his and our travels over the years. These journals also include ones he's kept about his times at home while I've been away, which has increasingly been the pattern. His cranky back, his inclination to hunker down, his lack of desire to see new things have kept him close to home, his books, and the company of a sequence of corgis.

I, TOO, HAVE KEPT JOURNALS of my and our travels, sometimes turning them into more formal pieces of writing, just as Bill has done. After our train trip to the West Coast in 1990, Bill published an essay about it in *The Hudson Review*. When my sister and I went to Sicily on a walking tour in 2005, I wrote a piece for our paper's magazine section. So I've been thinking: Why not interleave those journals and see what they say about us, about our travels, about traveling in general, about our marriage of six decades.

Our son Will says he thinks travel is one of the real tests of a marriage, a truism that happens to be true. He and his wife, Mo, have done a lot of traveling, living at times in the Central European countries where Mo, a historian, does her research. But he was thinking then of the wedding trip taken by his brother Mike and Mike's new wife, Kathy. They had been together importantly in each other's lives for about a decade, though living in different houses. They decided to celebrate their newly formalized union in an "ice resort" in Lapland, above the Arctic Circle. Here, the traveler can stay in an igloo with a glass ceiling and watch the Northern Lights up close. There is also a chilly-looking chapel where ceremonial observances take place. They went without hitch to Norway, where they stayed with a friend, then proceeded to Helsinki and from there to their resort some fifteen hundred miles farther north. All went smoothly until this point, and they evidently had a pleasant stay and a successful ceremony. The hitch came back home in the form of a monster snowstorm that nailed the Washington, D.C., area where they live. Flight out of Amsterdam canceled and Dulles airport, their destination, closed. How did they manage? They spent an extra day in Amsterdam, then got lucky and came into Dulles on its only open runway. Three feet of snow in Washington, where few people keep snow shovels in their vehicles. I try to imagine how they managed to uncover their car in the parking lot. Somehow they did, and Mike drove Kathy and the dog, a tall, elegant Afghan, which had been kenneled during their trip, up to their house in the country—where there was even more snow and an unshoveled driveway. Ah, yes, travel can be a test for sure.

For my parents—my father born in Budapest in 1895, my mother in Vienna in 1907—travel was an expression of their curiosity and wish to see the world, but also of their status as cultured, leisured people, with enough disposable income to spend on nonnecessities. Married in Budapest in 1931, they went on their honeymoon to Italy and to the Dalmatian coast of Croatia. They had a car with a chauffeur, stayed in good hotels, ate well. In the photo albums that I have of the first years of their marriage, there are many shots of monuments and churches, of my mother, always fashionably dressed, standing in front of one or another of these locations. (The chauffeur, Endre, later was said to have been responsible for denouncing their friends the Steiners, who were sheltered in our family's Budapest apartment near the end of the war. The Steiners were sent to Auschwitz, from where they never returned.)

After they came—*we* came, my parents, my sister, Doris

My parents, Eva and George Perl, were energetic travelers.
Based in Budapest, my father's hometown, they traveled
widely in Europe, sometimes with a car and chauffeur.
My father is at right in the lower picture.

(Dodo), and I—to the U.S. in 1939, just ahead of the out-
break of World War II, my parents traveled little. As "enemy
aliens"—Hungary had become an ally of Germany—they
couldn't easily leave the country. There was no going to
Europe until after the war, and they had little interest
in getting to know the States. Besides, there was gas
rationing. They had settled in Scarsdale, New York, on the
recommendation of a friend, an educator who vouched
for the public schools there. During the war they vacationed
at Lakewood, a comfortable resort in Skowhegan, Maine,
where there was a summer theater and a congenial artists'
colony. When the war was over, they returned to Europe,
visiting friends in Paris and Zurich, staying every summer
in the rather stuffy Margna Hotel in Sils Baselgia, a beautiful spot in a high Swiss valley. They took a tour to Greece
with a highbrow British group that included Agatha Christie,
her husband, Sir Max Mallowan, and Lord David Cecil.
And they visited Cuernavaca, Mexico, where friends had a
house. In her nineties my mother could still tell you about
the sites they visited and about their historical significance.
They had avoided Central Europe until the early 1960s,
when they made a brief visit to Austria and Hungary. My
father was reluctant to return to his home country, which
was now under Communist rule. No family members

remained there; all had emigrated or perished. But my mother wanted, as she said, "to draw a line under it." The experience was unpleasant. People were remote and formal. My father was convinced that their hotel room was bugged, and perhaps it was. The line my mother wanted was drawn, hard and fast. My parents never returned to Hungary after that, and I heard my father speak about it only once, when he was quite old. It was with friends of ours who had just spent a year there. "It was a beautiful country," my father said, and there were tears in his eyes.

As my parents grew older, they stopped going into the high mountains because of my father's heart condition, but went to several comfortable places in Italy with spa hotels. After his death, my mother returned once to the Margna Hotel, and even though some friends were also staying there, she felt awkward and lonely. She never went back.

Still, travel was always assumed to be a good thing. My sister continues this family tradition in an energetic way. Her husband, Charley, has a real wanderlust, combined with ongoing curiosity about the places he visits. He has worked in jobs that have taken him all around the world, and Dodo was able to accompany him to many of those places. They have kept on the move into old age, although the range of their travels has diminished somewhat.

ABOVE: *Bill's mother, Marion, visiting Olympia, Greece.*
BELOW: *My mother dressed properly for a flight.*

Bill's and my pattern has been different, with forays away from home contracting noticeably both in range and frequency as the years have gone by. Between 1964 and 1974, we and our sons spent three separate sabbatical years abroad. For quite a few years afterward, pretty much every other year, Bill and I traveled together in the summer, back to England several times, back to Italy several times, and then to France, where I wanted to follow the fatal trajectory of my Austrian grandfather, who died there at the hands of the Nazis in 1943.

In earlier years, Bill and I had made regular visits to the Boston/Cambridge area, where we still had many friends. We'd also had periodic stays in New York to go to the ballet, concerts and museums, walk miles of pavement, and eat in restaurants, things we did not do much at home in Amherst. We took summer vacations in various parts of New England—coastal Maine, Cape Cod, and for twenty years in a rented house in Westport, Massachusetts, on a tidal river near the coast.

Then, about a dozen years ago, Bill decided he did not want to travel anymore. I see the decision beginning with a diagnosis and treatment for prostate cancer in 2000, which put him in touch with his mortality in a new way. He was also beginning to have trouble with his back—not

*The cottage we rented for many years in Westport,
Massachusetts, looked out on the Westport River, home
to many varieties of birds, egrets among them.*

excruciating, but steady, chronic discomfort. Sitting in a car or an airplane for long periods was, to put it mildly, no fun. All of this appeared to concentrate his mind. From here on, he seemed to say, though not in so many words, he would spend his time and energy reading, writing, and teaching, listening to music and enjoying the meals in his kitchen, with me and sometimes with friends and family. No longer willing to drive to Boston to attend the basketball games in the now impossibly loud and expensive Garden, he would watch on TV as the Celtics' fortunes rose and fell. He would enjoy visits from his sons and grandchildren, staying home to keep our dog company while I periodically went to visit them and sometimes ventured even farther afield.

And so the journals we kept while traveling have come to represent for me not only accounts of our varied, often shared experiences, but also, in some larger way, our points of similarity and difference. I see them in combination as a portrait—a collage, a mosaic, a diptych—of our sixty-year-plus marriage. As a wickedly astute friend suggested, the title of this book should be *He Said, She Said*.

Bill and I married in 1957, and took a little wedding trip that included a couple of New England sites, a stop in the Adirondacks, where his family had vacationed early in his life, and then a few days at the excruciatingly elaborate

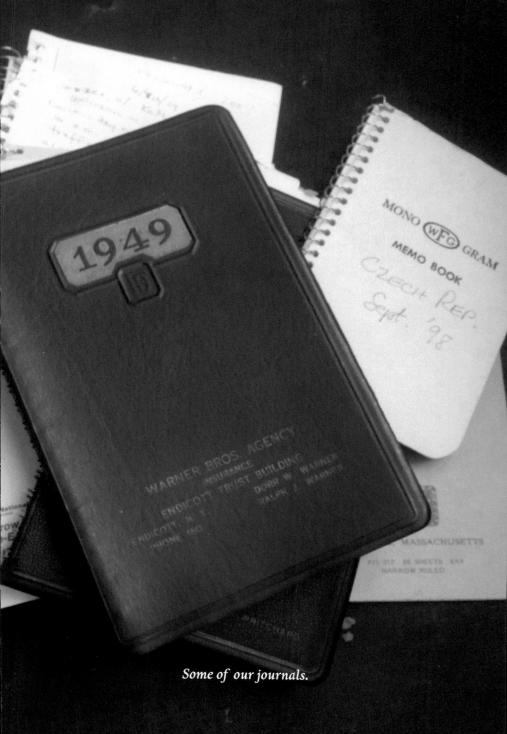

Some of our journals.

wedding of some friends. The following summer we rented a house on an island off the coast of Maine. It was isolated and beautiful. Bill brought his typewriter to work on his doctoral thesis, and I explored the island, learned to cook the mussels that grew on the rocks, swam—in brief, heroic spurts—in the frigid waters, and did a lot of reading. My mother, who visited at one point, remarked that this vacation would either result in a divorce or a pregnancy. Neither of these happened, although I did get pregnant the following year.

The first of our big trips was a sabbatical year in Rome, 1963–64. I was twenty-six and Bill thirty-one. We had two sons by then, ages three and eight months. I had been to Italy once before, with my parents as a teenager, sullen and resentful of having to be with them yet enjoying the country and testing my new knowledge of Italian art after a year in college. I was not a good traveling companion, since I was in a perpetual battle with my mother. I have a miniature plaster bas-relief, about the size of a large postcard, with a few horses and horsemen, a reproduction of a section of the Parthenon frieze. My father bought it for me in the little hilltown of Gubbio as a sort of effort at reconciliation, trying to bring me down off my high horse, perhaps. That visual pun could have been his if his

*Our first real vacation was on Sutton Island, Maine.
Bill set out with his typewriter, ready to work on his
dissertation. We had a number of visitors there, including
my sister, Dodo, and her husband-to-be, Charley Ablard,
who found a way to enjoy the rocky landscape.*

Hungarian-accented English had been good enough, but
in any case, this was the kind of gesture he believed in—
peacemaking gifts. It didn't work, of course, and it took
quite a few decades before I made something like real
peace with my mother.

Our sabbatical in Rome had none of the luxury of the
time I spent there with my parents, but we were comfortable enough in an apartment sublet from friends of friends.
Those friends had been persuasive about how much pleasure they'd had in Rome with their small children. Other
friends who had spent the previous year in England had
been equally persuasive. I did not experience that pleasure.
Instead, the year was a struggle to survive as a parent and a
wife. I was not good at making use of the people who could
have made things easier—a couple of British au pairs, one
after another, and an Italian housekeeper who came with
the apartment. I was young and not used to asking other
people to do things for me. It was all pre–women's movement, and I likewise did not know how to ask my husband
for help, much less an equal share of the work. So I tried to
do it all, and was angry and miserable. One friend, a single
man, a fellow at the American Academy in Rome, said to
me, disapprovingly, apropos of my lack of acquaintance
with important monuments: "You don't know where you

Rocky Point Inn was a full-service resort where Bill's family stayed for several weeks each summer from 1936 to 1949.

are." And he was surely right from his standpoint, that of a classics scholar who was being well looked after and had no domestic responsibilities. The accusation stung, and still stings. I was a bad tourist, a preoccupied visitor, not seeing what I was supposed to see. More than twenty years later, a couple of return trips to Italy without domestic obligations helped to rehabilitate my sense of that country and improve my standing as a conscientious traveler.

When he was growing up, Bill's family did not have the leisure or the money to travel, since his father, a lawyer for the Endicott-Johnson Shoe Company in Johnson City, New York, had only two weeks of vacation every year. His mother, a music supervisor in the public schools, had the long summer vacation, but funds were tight. From 1936 to 1949 that time was devoted to a family stay at Rocky Point Inn, a comfortable, full-service resort on Fourth Lake in the Adirondacks where they could enjoy three meals a day and the company of similar families. There was swimming (though Bill never really learned this, to my sorrow), tennis, hiking, boating, a pool table and ping-pong. Bill, a budding pianist, was encouraged to perform for an appreciative audience from a young age. Aside from that two-week sojourn, his father, a difficult and deeply dissatisfied man, truly had no interest in travel, although he agreed toward

RAILROAD SCHEDULES
Daily Except Sunday
Leave Grand Central, New York City,
8:30 A. M.
Arrive Thendara, 3:30 P. M.
Sleeper service, leave N. Y. C., 8:15 P. M.
Arrive Thendara, 4:10 A. M.
Leave Cleveland, Ohio, 5:45 A. M.
Leave Buffalo, 10:00 A. M.
Leave Rochester, 11:14 A. M.
Arrive Thendara, 3:30 P. M.
Sleeper Service
Leave Buffalo 10:00 P. M., Rochester 11:14
P. M., Arrive Thendara 4:10 A. M.

	Rd. Trip	1-Way
New York City	$13.23	$7.34
Cleveland, Ohio	17.71	11.07
Rochester	9.03	4.75
Buffalo	11.56	6.39
Syracuse	5.06	2.66
Albany	7.13	3.74
Philadelphia, Pa.		9.63

Hotel taxi meets all trains on notification.
No charge for transportation to hotel, including baggage.
Guests who come by train or bus are assured of ample local transportation.
Bus schedules to and from Utica furnished on request.
Specific inquiries on nature of clientele gladly answered.

RATE SCHEDULE, 1945

ROCKY POINT INN

High in the Central Adirondack Mountains on Fourth Lake, P. O. Inlet, N. Y.

Hamilton County   Accommodates 150

A. G. DELMARSH, *owner-manager*

Offering rest and recreation from June until October, located directly on lakeshore one mile from village in which are located cinema, stores, etc., BOTH CATHOLIC AND PROTESTANT CHURCHES.

Telephone service—daily mails—air and taxi service—life guard at bathing beach.

Average summer water temperature 68 degrees.

Lake Altitude 1700 feet.

MIDSEASON RATES

HOTEL	COTTAGES

Weekly

Rooms with Running Water
For one, $42.00 and $49.00
For two, $84.00 and $98.00

Rooms with Private Bath
For one, $56.00 through $98.00
For two, $126.00

Daily

Rooms with Running Water
For one, $7.00 and $8.00
For two, $14.00 through $16.00

Rooms with Private Bath
For one, $9.00 through $15.00
For two, $20.00

Rates include meals, entertainment, and all Inn facilities except golf, boats, and riding.
Golf— $1.50 per day at Inlet Golf Course; $2.00 per day, $10.00 per week at Thendara Golf Course.
Riding— From $1.00 to $2.00 per hour, varies with stables.
Canoes, rowboats— $1.50 per day, $6.00 per week. Outboards, sailboats, motorboats, on request.
Garage— $1.00 per night, $5.00 per week.

Rooms with Running Water
For one, $49.00
For two, $84.00 through $98.00
Rooms with Private Bath
For one, $56.00 through $105.00
For two, $98.00 through $140.00
Individual Cottages on Sand Beach
For one, $105.00   For three, $245.00
For two, $140.00   For four, $280.00

Rooms with Running Water
For one, $8.00
For two, $14.00 through $16.00

Rooms with Private Bath
For one, $9.00 through $16.00
For two, $18.00 through $22.00

Individual Cottages on Sand Beach
For one, $20.00   For three, $40.00
For two, $22.00   For four, $44.00

Special family rates on request.
Children under ten occupying parents' room, one-half single rate.

We welcome specific inquiries concerning our clientele.

From September 6 until October 1, ten percent reduction on above rates.

Useful information from the Rocky Point Inn, 1945.

Bill (right) and one of the boys in the band that traveled to Europe in 1951 to play for the U.S. troops there.

the end of his too-short life to go with his wife to the Canadian West, where they visited Banff and Lake Louise. Bill's mother, a woman of boundless energy into extreme old age, had, by contrast, always wanted to see the world, and had made one lengthy car trip west in her early fifties with a friend and their two younger children. Later, after retiring, she went on tours that took her around the world, touching many of the most famous tourist spots, registering her approval or disapproval of them, much as she did for everything in the rest of her life. She came to visit us when we were on sabbatical. A less-than-pleasant cruise to the Bahamas from her retirement home in Florida when she was in her late nineties was the last of her trips.

Bill had been to Europe in 1951 as a college student, traveling with a jazz band that was hired to entertain troops. But although they touched down and performed in many spots, from Frankfurt and Vienna to Casablanca and Rabat, they were not exactly tourists. They were there to perform, not to see the sights. When he and I and our two very small children got to Rome in 1963, he was ready to learn about the place. The *Blue Guide* became his bible, and he followed its instructions and often quoted its severe opinions: "A not very impressive ravine" was one of our favorites. This habit of consulting guidebooks continued through our next two sabbatical tours, both of them in London, where Pevsner's architectural observations became his new source of truth. On our travels, I was often the one who was seeing oddities not necessarily in the guidebook. I took photos of a series of doorbells in Florence, stone walls in Westport, Massachusetts. "Look!" I was often exhorting him—and still do at times—as he kept and keeps his nose planted firmly in the guidebook or some other volume.

Later, Bill shelved his guidebooks and agreed to come with me on some of my efforts to put together a family history, efforts that resulted in my book *Among Strangers*, published in 2010. I find now that rather than visiting tourist attractions when I travel, I prefer to have or invent a reason for going, a project I can work on. Sometimes there have been pilgrimages to places where people from my past have lived and died, and sometimes there have been experiences I wanted to try and then to write about— the walking tour in Sicily with my sister was one.

For the past few years—really since 2010—I'd been thinking about death and dying as I put together my book *The Way to Go: Portrait of a Residential Hospice*. Except for some public appearances at libraries and perhaps the prospect of an e-book, I'm done with that subject for now. So I've moved the death books from the little two-foot shelf near my desk and have made room for the travel books. These are not the guidebooks we've collected over the years, but a sort of meta-travel collection—books about travel, about travelers, by travelers. I've repurchased a copy of Alain de Botton's book *The Art of Travel*, which had disappeared (I must have lent it to someone). I had found it quirky and delightful, and am finding it so again. Hard not to quote endlessly from it. Right at the start, he gets my attention with a dreamy trip to Barbados inspired by a seductive brochure. Here he finds the real place to be quite different from what he expected, but pleasant nonetheless. Then he has a dispute with the woman he calls M., his travel companion/lover, and everything changes. Our capacity for enjoyment, he says, seems to depend on our emotional needs, among them the needs "for love, expression and respect. Thus we will not enjoy—we are not *able* to enjoy—sumptuous tropical gardens and attractive wooden beach huts when a relationship to which we are committed abruptly reveals itself to be suffused with incomprehension and resentment." Remember our son Will's comment that travel is a real test of a relationship. Yes indeed.

We have to learn how to travel together, just as we have to learn how to live together in the same house. There is a huge difference between them, however. At home we develop routines and familiarities: work, friends, landscapes, foods, knowledge of how to get things done—cars serviced, illnesses diagnosed. When we travel we leave those habits, those friends, that landscape and that know-how behind. That's the point, of course, to take ourselves out of the habitual, to enlarge our horizons. Travel, as the old cliché used to have it, is broadening. What we seek is that experience of being stretched, of making it new. Yet as with other kinds of stretching, there is perhaps no gain without a bit of pain. All of us have our definitions of what constitutes too much pain. Will we climb Everest with sherpas? Travel twenty-four hours to New Zealand? Ride crowded trains in India? Stay in airless hotels in New York? Where do we draw the line?

So, what do I know now about how to travel with Bill? I know that no matter how long or short the trip, when we arrive at our destination, he will immediately want to take a nap. Meanwhile, I will want to go out and walk. This is as true for a morning's drive to New York City or Boston as it is for an overnight flight to London or Rome. We go our separate ways on arrival and reconvene later. We have learned to do the same in museums—look at the clock and set a time to meet up, then wander freely or together as seems best.

Alain de Botton is nothing if not literary. He quotes

at some length from Baudelaire, whose poem "L'Invitation au Voyage" promises a destination where everything would provide *"ordre et beauté/Luxe, calme et volupté"* (order and beauty/Luxury, calm and delight). But the story of travel for Baudelaire, as for many travelers, is the story of disappointment. De Botton, by contrast, has discovered a destination so undemanding and familiar that it never disappoints. He's a Londoner, and when he wants another point of view, he heads for Heathrow Airport.

> When feeling sad at home, I have often boarded a train or airport bus and gone to Heathrow, where, from an observation gallery in Terminal 2 or from the top floor of the Renaissance Hotel along the north runway, I have drawn comfort from the sight of the ceaseless landing and takeoffs of aircraft.

I, too, have found some comfort in airports, though I've never tried seeking one out when I wasn't flying somewhere. Still, I can see de Botton's point. Especially when I'm alone and not worrying about someone else's needs and comfort, once I arrive at the gate, I can settle into a sort of alert meditative state, if that's not a contradiction in terms. I am waiting for my plane, but am powerless

to do anything about it, so I can read or even write with
concentration, walk up and down the long hallways, or
peacefully eat the sandwich I've brought along to stave off
the hunger we can all anticipate on plane trips these days.

A different sort of pleasure is described by Willa Cather
in one of her letters from abroad written for a newspaper
in Lincoln, Nebraska, on her first trip out of the U.S. She
has already been in some big cities and visited some well-
known sites, but finds herself now in a place that few have
heard of, Le Lavandou, in Provence, discovering an aston-
ishing feeling of delight.

> Out of every wandering in which people and places
> come and go in long successions, there is always one
> place remembered above the rest because the exter-
> nal or internal conditions were such that they most
> nearly produced happiness. I am sure that for me that
> one place will always be Lavandou. Nothing else in
> England or France has given anything like this sense
> of immeasurable possession and immeasurable con-
> tent. I am sure I do not know why a wretched little
> fishing village, with nothing but green pines and blue
> sea and a sky of porcelain, should mean more than
> a dozen places that I have wanted to see all my life.
> No books have ever been written about Lavandou,

no music or pictures ever came from her but I know
well enough that I shall yearn for it long after I have
forgotten London and Paris. One cannot divine nor
forecast the conditions that will make happiness; one
only tumbles upon them by chance, in a lucky hour,
at the world's end somewhere, and holds fast to the
days, as to fortune or fame.

Both de Botton and Cather describe a sense of peace and
comfort in the locations they have traveled to. But Cather
suggests something else too—that Le Lavandou will be a
place she will remember after the memories of more famous
places have faded. I had felt something of this sensation
when I traveled with Bill to Hungary on my second trip
there, this time coming close to what I was looking for—a
property on the Great Plain of Hungary that had belonged
to my great-grandfather. I wrote about this surprising—or
perhaps predictable—feeling in *Among Strangers*, the book I
wrote about my family. Someone I barely knew had asked
me whether, although I'd lived in Amherst for most of my
life, I'd ever felt really at home somewhere.

"Yes," I said, "on the plains of Hungary." And as I
said it, it felt right, even though I'd never put it just
that way before. Later, in a more reflective moment,

I decided that feeling at home may be a little like fall-
ing in love, both of them connected to precipitous
and distinct sensations, both dangerously tinged with
myth, cliché and longing.

The Great Hungarian Plain, the Alföld or *puszta*,
begins in Budapest, just east of the Danube, as soon
as you cross one of the many bridges connecting the
green hills of Buda with the flat bustling center of
Pest. Keep heading east and the land stays flat, the
sky huge. Go east another 100 kilometers and you will
reach Hungary's other major river, the Tisza, an often
muddy, sluggish stream that runs roughly parallel to
the Danube before joining it in the former Yugosla-
via. You will have passed through some of the richest
land on our planet, flat and fertile, a dark, alluvial soil
capable of growing almost anything . . .

In 1991, I had headed out this way with my husband. As I exclaimed over the beauties of the landscape, Bill hunched further down behind the steering
wheel, resisting my efforts to include him in my quest
for family footprints. He was not moved by the red-
tile-roofed villages or the acres of vineyards, nor the
rows of poplars lining the small country roads. He
was not enjoying the hot sun and the flatness. He was
not amused when we had to wait most of an hour on
a dusty riverbank to put our rented car on a rickety
raft-like ferry to take us across the Tisza River.

As I note in that book, Bill has had all the roots he ever needed or wanted in his upstate New York upbringing, so he never quite understood my need to search for mine. But that didn't fully account for his reluctance and irritability in the Hungarian countryside. It was more about not being a good sport, not being a Boy Scout, unlike my attempts to roll with the punches, expect the unexpected, as my teenage travels with the Experiment in International Living had taught me. His spirit of adventure was distinctly limited. This was not *fun*! It made him anxious and he was not going to conceal it.

OF COURSE ANXIETY is one of the hallmarks of travel. I'm inclined to think that this is not altogether a bad thing, a kind of stage fright that is perhaps beneficial, opening our eyes and ears to sights and sounds in ways that don't happen in ordinary life. I take my twice-yearly half an Ambien the night before travels, and that keeps the anticipatory anxiety at bay. It's not necessarily better sleeping, I've found, but it keeps me from fussing. If I'd been planning to fly after the latest terrorist attack in an airport, I might have had some real anxieties, but mostly they are ephemeral, trivial: Will the alarm go off? Do I have the passport in my pocketbook? Will I get enough sleep? No question, there is plenty to worry about as you set out to leave home. First of all there's the house and the dog. A house-/dog-sitter can take care of both of those, but that person needs to be available and reliable. We have stopped putting our dog in our nice vet's boarding kennel, finding that for the price, we can get a twofer that covers all the bases, leaving the dog in familiar surroundings while removing worries about floods, power outages and missed garbage collections.

Then there's the question of what to bring. Pack and unpack, more shoes, fewer shoes, bigger suitcase, smaller suitcase. How can I be warm enough, cool enough, comfortable enough, and still remain presentable? I like to challenge myself to see how little I can travel with, following the admirable example of my friend Fran, who always traveled, no matter how far and for how long, with only a carry-on suitcase. She took only black and white clothes, with a few colorful scarves for variety. She took two pairs of shoes, one for serious walking and the other, still comfortable but a little dressier. I have recently acquired a mini wheeled carry-on, which I tried out on a weekend visit to my sister. It worked fine, and I may try it when I visit our son and family in Oregon. It even fits easily in an airport bathroom stall—one of the requirements if you're traveling alone.

Bill expresses his travel anxieties with tiredness, needing many extra hours of sleep before departing, a long nap upon arriving. He was pleased to encounter a piece by John Updike about a visit to Finland. Updike, who tended to be determinedly cheerful, showed himself here as a fellow sufferer.

> I take an interest in hotel rooms. To the man travelling alone, his hotel room, first entered in rumpled clothes, with a head light from sleeplessness, looms as the arena where he will suffer insomnia, constipation, loneliness, nightmares, and telephone calls [here he describes the layout and furniture of the room] . . . The closet coat hangers were especially progressive abstract sculptures of white plastic it took some practice to manipulate. One's hotel room is a place one is always trying to leave and yet always returning to. Staying in it, alone with the television set, seems cowardly and a waste of the airplane ticket, and yet leaving it, stepping into the long, windowless, carpeted hall, letting the door click shut as you tap your pocket to make sure the key is there has a sadness, too, the sadness of rejecting a symbolic mother, a place that would serve as home.

He goes to bed early, then wakes up and can't get back to sleep. He speaks of the "bone-deep self-estrangement of jet lag," insomnia with its attendant agitation.

> The precariousness of being alive and human was no longer hidden from me by familiar surroundings and the rhythm of habit. I was fifty-five, ignorant, dying, and filling this bit of Finland with the smell of my stale sweat and insomniac fury.

Later, he heads out, buys a hat and umbrella, and feels more cheerful.

> As a child, I used to wonder whether or not I would live to the year 2000. It seemed incredibly far away. Now, here in Finland, I sat gray-haired among unintelligibly chatting teen-agers who had every expectation of entering the twenty-first century. I was happy in their company. The two national treats tourists are expected to savor—taking a sauna and eating reindeer meat—I had managed to avoid, but I had survived my nights in hotel rooms, and I had brought sunlight to this waterlogged land by the simple act of buying an umbrella. I had seen the lakes and forests. I had filled in another blank space in the coloring book of the world.

The coloring book of the world. Ah, yes. Not everyone wants to visit all those blank spaces. But as Proust famously said in *Remembrance of Things Past*, in reference to the difference it makes to look at the world through the work of different artists and musicians: "The only true voyage of discovery, the only fountain of Eternal Youth, would be not to visit strange lands but to possess other eyes, to behold the universe through the eyes of another, of a hundred others, to behold the hundred universes that each of them beholds."

In other words, as Bill would say: Stay home and read a book.

1990. Bill waits at the Flagstaff, Arizona, station before heading by bus for the Grand Canyon. The map shows the route of the Lake Shore Limited as far as Chicago, which we took on our way out west. Coming back we took the southern route.

Train to the West

I N APRIL OF 1990, Bill and I boarded a train in Springfield, Massachusetts, and headed to the West Coast. We went via Chicago, Denver, and Salt Lake City to Seattle, stopping overnight in Chicago and Salt Lake City, where we were shown around in each place by former students of Bill's. This was a good way to manage the trip, since it gave us the long train ride plus a couple of interspersed nights with a real bed and a real shower. At the end of the ride, we stopped for several days in Seattle, where we stayed with good friends of our own age. On the return trip, we flew to San Francisco, where we visited more former students of Bill's, then went on to Berkeley to see more old friends. The Berkeley couple, we learned from our friends in Seattle, were on the verge of divorce, though this was not mentioned during our lively, talky evening with them. We were not supposed to know.

From San Francisco, we went to Los Angeles to catch Amtrak's southern route, via the Grand Canyon, then to St. Louis, Chicago, and back to Springfield, a trip of three weeks, one of our longest times away from home except for our sabbaticals in Italy and England.

As Bill and I wrote about our experience, our accounts converged and diverged in often predictable and, I think, amusing ways. Bill's version takes us all the way to the very end, when we arrive at the Springfield station. Mine, for some reason, peters out in Flagstaff, Arizona, where we had just seen the Grand Canyon. Was I exhausted by that famous and amazing sight? Who knows?

Bill's journal is typed—typically, since writing by hand is not comfortable for him. In 1990 he was typing on an IBM Selectric, as he had for years and as he continues to do even now, although in the past few years he has converted to a computer for the final copies of his essays and reviews. Did he keep notes of our three-week sojourn? He doesn't think so. He wrote it all down after we returned. I am impressed, as always, by his capacity for recall, his detailed remembrance of names, places and events—especially meals—past. My own recollections are recorded contemporaneously in one of a series of spiral-bound notebooks. For many years I had the habit of starting a different one for each trip. Recently I've become more frugal of paper, combining several excursions in a single notebook.

Here is how Bill's account of that trip west begins:

Sunday, April 8: Springfield, Mass., to Albany, N.Y.

The problem was how to get through this day (without a Celtics game) until train departure time at 7:40 p.m. This was somehow managed, and David picked us up, took us to the station (providing useful help with heavy suitcases, not soon again to be available—the help, that is).

I am aware here already of Bill's steady sense of the possibilities of loss (the Celtics) and difficulties (lugging suitcases in the absence of a sturdy son). Bill's stance toward the world and his life has always reminded me of a Housman poem from *A Shropshire Lad*, one of many pieces of poetry he has introduced me to:

> *I to my perils*
> *Of cheat and charmer*
> *Came clad in armour*
> *By stars benign.*
> *Hope lies to mortals*
> *And most believe her*
> *But man's deceiver*
> *Was never mine.*
> *The thoughts of others*
> *Were light and fleeting,*

Of lovers' meeting
Or luck or fame.
Mine were of Trouble,
And mine were steady,
So I was ready
When Trouble came.

Well, of course he wasn't always ready when trouble came. His motto was not the Boy Scout's "Be Prepared"; rather he was always anticipating difficulties—accentuating the negative, you might say—but without anticipating a solution. He was Eeyore in *Winnie-the-Pooh*, or the pessimist in the old joke about the optimist and the pessimist: Parents have two sons. One is always happy and cheerful; the other is just the opposite, always gloomy. How are they to understand this? A psychiatrist gives them a test. He puts the pessimist in a room full of brand-new toys and games, and after a while he comes in to find the boy weeping bitterly. "What's the matter?" asks the shrink. "Oh," says the boy, "these things are wonderful, but they're going to get old and break and the pieces will get lost." The psychiatrist then visits the optimist, who he's put in a room full of horse manure. The little boy is laughing and happily tossing the stuff up in the air.

What's the explanation? "With all this shit," says the little boy, "there must be a pony in here somewhere."

Bill will insist that this tendency toward the dark side reflects his perspective as a satirist, and when it's amusing I can see his point, but it can also be just plain irritating. My own stance is the less amusing one of the problem solver: What can I do about this? Which is not to say that I don't complain, but usually after I'm done doing that, I try to see if the problem can be solved, and if it can't, I usually try to shut up and turn my attention elsewhere.

But the next few sentences in Bill's journal turn his attention to the plus side:

> The expected feeling of relief on plunking ourselves down in an agreeably spacy and not yet odorous coach seat was nonetheless welcome, even though predicted. Better yet, we had followed Bill Kennick's instructions about not eating supper till on the train. Since there's no diner between Springfield and Albany, we were prepared with a Picnic Supper, ham and chicken sandwiches following martini drunk from brother Craig's silver cup (or so I term it). It was dark, there was nothing to look at, so we blundered along happily on the first leg of things. Sometime after 11 p.m., we disgorged at the Albany (actually Rensselaer) station,

spanking new, and waited for placement on the Lake
Shore Limited . . . We were eventually placed in what
is known euphemistically as a Slumber Coach, in the
intricacies of which we were instructed by the most
interesting Train Attendant encountered on the trip.
This was Dick Holt, a retired dentist, who, after thirty
years, so he said, of not being sued by patients, decided
it was time for a new career. His aspirations are to
procure a place on the Chicago-to-west-coast Zephyr.

In my journal I note that our dentist/attendant gives
us tips on where to sit, including to position ourselves on
the right when crossing the Mississippi in order to see the
whole train turning. We take his advice. Bill goes on:

The lounge car having been opened up as the train
headed west of Albany, and with both of us reluctant
to go to bed and face up to the Slumber Coach's sleeping terms, I got a beer (the only one I purchased on
Amtrak) and we talked until tired. Having converted
the "room" (it consists of two small facing seats and a
tiny sink and toilet, right at your elbow), we distributed
ourselves in the beds, me at first in the upper. No go.
I simply didn't fit (too long for it) and Marietta kindly
exchanged with me. So ended the first few hours.

We arrive in Chicago after a restless night, but before that, Bill is cheered by the hearty breakfast.

Nothing brings things round like breakfast. Amtrak breakfasts, as well as their other meals, turned out to be first-rate: nicely done eggs, good breakfast "meats" (bacon and sausage), even grits a couple of times on the more southern routes. Lunch, which is a free-for-all (one makes reservations for dinner) was less appealing, but equipped with Vouchers (our food having been paid for in advance, as it were), it was pleasant not to think abut prices and just dig in.

An important aspect of train dining is that you are seated—almost invariably, since the train is usually crowded, as this first one was—opposite another couple, so there is more or less the obligation to make conversation: Where are you headed, where do you live, is this your first trip, etc. Marietta's absolute willingness to engage in such conversation made it easier on me, who could be counted upon, nonetheless, to produce the occasional monosyllabic grunt of assent. Anyway we had no disastrous table companions and indeed some lively ones.

Helen Deutsch, our Chicago hostess, is not at her apartment when we arrive, so we sit on her doorstep in the drizzle for a while. When she gets there, Bill tucks in for a nap. A little late afternoon drinks party has been arranged, with Cheryl Young, an old friend, mainly of Bill's, and two academic types, both teaching at Northwestern, Alfred Appel and Joe Epstein. The two men arrive first, and Bill describes the scene:

> Lively and humorous talk, as might be expected, and it was not dampened by the arrival of Cheryl. For a while I thought her changed, more modulated and reasonable, but that was a momentary illusion. She had read some Henry James and found him basically a terrible writer—an asshole. So she announced to Joe Epstein, who had just finished describing to us his current course in Henry James at Northwestern. A further indiscreet remark by Cheryl concerning Epstein's wife—nothing personal, but still—made for a rough moment. Epstein was courteous and Cheryl withdrew somewhat. After the Northwestern boys left, we went out to an excellent Italian restaurant.

Here Bill neglects to mention what I have included: "Excellent dinner follows at Sole Mio, where Cheryl dumps a glass of wine on me, then blames me for making her feel gauche. (My formulation to Helen next morning: She cuts through a lot of crap, but she also creates a lot of crap.)"

Next day Helen takes us around to see the sights, first various ethnic neighborhoods: Ukrainian, Hispanic, etc. Then the Art Institute. The next is from my journal:

Tuesday is free at the Art Institute, so full of people—a fine place. Exhibits of Chicago architecture—Sullivan and Wright. Also plenty of excellent Impressionists. Just getting started on Old Masters when it's time to go to Berghoff's for lunch. [Bill's favorite place.]

Splendid, fast, all-male service in dark downstairs section of this heavy German place—sauerbraten, pork loin, sausages, potato pancakes, creamed spinach, beer. Service in about 8 minutes. Helen gets us to the station after a few misses. Crammed waiting room. First-class waiting room not much better, but all service and announcements very efficient, well-handled.

We ride in royal splendor in our Deluxe Sleeper across Illinois and Missouri into Iowa. Beautiful open farmland, black soil recently plowed, little towns meet the railroad. Amazing expanse—flat, endless, sparsely settled. Occasional big farmhouses with trees looking like oases in a fertile desert. The sun goes down and a big moon comes up over the not-quite heartland. Hungarian [I am studying the language and have brought books with me] a pleasant diversion, but I

hate to do it when there's a view. Also P. D. James. I sit
in the coach after dinner because it's too crowded for
two to read and write in our compartment once the
beds are down.

Reading and writing is what Bill and I do a lot of in the
rest of our lives, when we're not eating or sleeping. I have
a longer list of other things I do, but for Bill, along with
teaching, music, and watching his favorite sports teams,
this *is* his life. His 2015 collection of essays and reviews is
titled, appropriately, *Writing to Live*. Other people might
worry about what clothing to bring on a trip. He mainly
concentrates on what books to bring.

Reading is not easy aboard Amtrak [he writes on
April 10, in his section titled "Chicago to the Wilds
of Iowa"], and I think not because I've selected the
wrong books to bring along. I had been warned both
by my mother and Theodore Baird [former teacher,
now colleague and friend] not to overequip myself
with reading matter, but to look out the window.
But it seems fair to disregard the advice after dark.
Tonight, however, I did poorly at holding my eyes on
the correct line of type as the train jounced about. I
brought along the most irrelevant titles: a late Trollope,

Mr. Scarborough's Family; Howells's *A Hazard of New Fortunes;* P. D. James's *Innocent Blood;* and Johnson's *Lives of the Poets.* We'll see what happens.

Wednesday, April 11: Iowa to Salt Lake City

Yesterday's crossing, before dusk, of the Mississippi into Burlington, Iowa, was interesting because the Iowa town was nicely un-Iowan, hilly, rather old-fashioned and dark in construction, plenty of trees. This morning Marietta reported that, when she looked out during the night, it was snowing in Omaha. That's all we have to say about Nebraska. When we woke early, we were just east of Denver, in a truly godforsaken part of Colorado, very bad badlands with nothing except mean soil, used cars, falling-down shacks. Very grim Americana. We got off the train at Denver, which seemed slightly unreal as a town, just plunked down there somehow, walked six blocks or so away from, then back to the station. (We were instructed not to leave the station precincts, but daringly disobeyed.)

This would be unquestionably the great scenery day, following the Colorado River for much of it, through the gorges, then coming into Utah and the red rocks. Amtrak's strongest selling point, this section.

So that was Bill's description of the scenery. Mine was more detailed:

From Denver—where fog and clouds obscure the
mountains—the train climbs slowly up the east side
of the Rockies. Ice coats needles of Ponderosa pines,
snow first in patches, then more snow. Frequent tun-
nels, switchbacks with great views. No wildlife all day,
except cows later on (not so wild), though we were
promised elk and "jackalope." Then back down the
other side as we follow the path of the Colorado River
for many miles. Spectacular canyons, some red rock
with grainy layers like some immense piece of pastry,
some gray and rounded, like animal forms, or even
anthropomorphic. Small settlements along river sug-
gest old mining communities, log-sided houses. One
huge piece of highway being built along river—said
to be the most expensive ever. Territory flattens out
as we reach Utah. Near Thompson (a stop), we sit for
1½ hours while a freight train on our tracks works out
a coupling problem. As the sun sets in a fine show of
silver and pink on the "book cliffs" on one side, open
bare range on the other, a fast-moving black cloud
passes through, moves on. We're late coming in at
Salt Lake, and it's half past midnight when a slightly
boozy cab driver takes us to the Little America, where
we fall into the immense round tub and big white bed.

Bill has provided a little more information here about how
the creature comfort of the hotel contrasts with the train.

This was the first point at which the relief from train-
grubbiness seemed a thing to appreciate. My attempt
to take a shower aboard Amtrak was pitiful. They
advise you to sit down in the coffin-like toilet area
("If you must stand, hold on to the ???" [Bill here not
remembering what he was being told to hold on to])
and then press the shower button, at which time some
drops of water will leak out from the instrument you
are holding over some part of you. This less-than-
satisfactory wetting continues for only about 20 sec-
onds. It is also possible—though we did not make the
mistake—to press the shower button rather than the
toilet flusher, causing the user of the toilet to become
wetter than he or she desired.

Bill's former student Jill Maney was to pick us up in the
afternoon, so we had the morning to ourselves. Bill writes:

We spent the morning, a warm one, walking the 8 or
9 long blocks which take you to Temple Square, where
we inspected things Mormonesque. Not of great interest, I found, and one is subject at any moment to the
approach of one of the faithful, intent upon helping
one out with some not so subtle proselytizing. The
male elders tend to look like Selah Tarrant ("Want to
try a little inspiration?") out of *The Bostonians*. The
young girls who lead the tours are scrubbed and

vigorous, though somewhat lacking in allure. They
testify; they're satisfied.

We walked over to the Salt Palace and Marietta
inquired as to seats that night between the Jazz–
Lakers. Sold out since November, the expected answer.
A walk back to the hotel, carefully observing injunc-
tions not to cross against the lights despite a complete
lack of traffic in all directions. You could get arrested
for that, no doubt, in S.L.C.

Some additional comments from me:

After half a day, I said to Bill, I want to see a really
slutty-looking woman. How 'bout a little Eastern
snarl? Big wide streets, every intersection with well-
designed sloping curb for disabled, traffic lights that
chirp in different keys for pedestrians. Much of down-
town overbuilt, now for rent, lots of vacant buildings
(as in Denver, we later learn).

Temple Square, where Mormons concentrate, the
Temple, only open to certified Mormons, the museum,
the info center, the Tabernacle. Everyone oozing
officious friendliness, wants to put us on mailing
lists. Young woman giving spiel to foreign tourists,
lists all places they're from: This group is from
Germany (applause, yay!), this from Sweden (yay,

applause!), and a group from Seattle (applause, etc.).
And my partner, she says, pointing to a small dark-
haired, non-Midwest person, is from Rome, Italy
(small yays), so you'll have to excuse her accent. All
this was being watched from across the way by a
sinister-looking too-friendly white-haired man in
a blue suit and an older, thinner, worn version of the
fresh young woman. Jill later shows us Brigham
Young's "dormitory," a big house where he lived with
40-some wives. In the square, flowers—tulips, daffs,
huge pansies—in rigid perfect bloom. I think I detect
some artificial scent, but maybe it's just the tourists.

Bill reports that Jill, "looking good" (no Mormon, she),
picked us up and took us to a couple of ski resorts. He also
notes that "As preparation for the Grand Canyon, I felt only
mildly upset with the heights." (He suffers from vertigo.)
We went to supper, heard that the Jazz had upset the Lakers,
then walked over to the Tabernacle and listened to a
rehearsal of the choir. "This was pleasant and efficiently
done," writes Bill. Back to the hotel for a farewell drink
with Jill, and we showed up for the 11:30 train heading for
Seattle. Bill writes:

Friday, April 12

Breakfast was taken in the neighborhood of Boise, Idaho, where nature came on in full profusion. Trees heavily budded, like Amherst in mid-May—I hadn't expected this. (Seattle was to be similarly advanced.) This train didn't seem terribly crowded, and in the afternoon we left our deluxe roomette for an even better (and nonobservational) car and perched in one of the economy rooms with two seats facing each other. This proved to be a very good place to watch the splendors of the Columbia River as we moved through The Dalles and the salmon fisheries toward Portland. One felt one had seen almost enough Spectacular Nature for a while, and I became very impatient to arrive at Seattle and a few days off the train.

We pulled in about an hour and a half late, in the rain, smack up against the Kingdome, where the Mariners had just played their opener. Roger and Dorothy [the Sales] picked us up, and after sampling some of Seattle's finest beer in their redecorated kitchen [a "new blue kitchen, $80,000," I note], we piled into bed.

Saturday, April 14, Seattle

Good to get sorted out and to cut one's nails (one of the only things I'd forgotten to bring along was my trusty nail clipper). We prevailed upon Roger to drive us to the Pike Place Market, where a profusion of fish and beautiful asparagus and aggressively red rhubarb regaled us. We purchased salmon and Dungeness crab for next night's dinner, then had an excellent lunch at a Bolivian (yes) restaurant overlooking the market. A crush of people, very agreeable food—some sort of shrimp soup with good bread. We walked a bit in the splendid Seattle sunny weather. Roger and I assessed the current state of literary criticism (he has no further interest in T. S. Eliot, is mainly preoccupied with revising his novel) and other matters. His old friends Jack and Midge Brenner for dinner, steamed clams and a stir-fry, prepared by Rog.

Sunday, April 15, Seattle

Easter Sunday morning and the Sales went to some sort of bible instruction group, then came back and picked up Marietta for the "church" service, which I didn't have a second thought about finessing. Nobody attempted to keep me from watching the Celtics, who were indeed on the tube with the Knicks at the Boston Garden, 10 a.m. Seattle time. Celts at the top of their game, at least for much of it, left the Knicks in the dust and things looked good for the future. Little did we know.

Meanwhile, I attended church with the Sales and a small breakaway group (this is why Bill put quotes around "church") that had decided the Presbyterians were too

hidebound, too something for them. Roger refers to his
congregation as the Busted Believers (this is also the title
of his novel). My journal records the event.

> Young curly-dishevelled-haired minister in a flowered
> dress. Congregation of 8, including me. A moving
> moment—a slim, elegant black man holds up a green
> Easter egg, tells about a three-year-old girl who has
> given it to him. It's a dingy neighborhood with shoot-
> ings at school, but some signs of hope.
>
> We're in the lobby of a little theater. The altar is the
> concession stand counter—beer, wines, soft drinks.
> Minister's (Jewish) significant other plays trumpet for
> our hymns. A touching occasion. She sermonizes vs.
> stodgy Presbyterians (she's one), exhorts in favor of
> rejoicing, bright colors.
>
> Afterwards, walked in the Arboretum, heard Doro-
> thy's life story. Excellent eating at Saleses'—seafood
> stir-fry, cut-up fruit salad with lemon chiffon on top,
> then salmon grilled on new stove.

That night, our mutual friend, Paul Alpers, called to tell
Roger that he and his wife Svetlana were separating, but
that for the present we (who were to have supper with
them on Thursday) were not to know. This seemed, as Bill
put it mildly, an awkward situation.

Next day, Bill went to sit in on Roger's "very good and personable" class. Bill writes: "I asked him whether his classes were always that good—I hoped not." Dorothy and I took ourselves to the city where we ate fried clams and chips along with the seagulls and small kids on the waterfront. We visited the Museum of History and Industry, where there were exhibits on fitness, clothes and old Seattle streets. We moseyed around in shops, agreeing that our husbands were no good at this kind of desultory retail-based activity.

I check in with Mother in Amherst every few days. She reports that she's "lonely," but otherwise fine. (She is eighty-three and living alone in the condo where she and my father moved six years ago.) She will leave for my sister's in Alexandria, Virginia, at the end of the week.

I try to think of how to respond to Roger's "novel." I write: "I try to be both frank and kind—not easy. There's a lot of religious stuff, and his effort to be a nice regular guy is a problem."

Bill visits the Eliot Bay Bookstore and reports that there's no sign of his new book, *Randall Jarrell: A Literary Life*. Another meal and a night at the Saleses' before we head for San Francisco, this time via air rather than rail. An unpleasantly crowded limo ride from the airport with an equally unpleasant driver lands us at the supremely pleasant Inn at Union Square. Small, cozy, full of appealing amenities—continental breakfast with fresh hot breads, tea in the afternoon, followed by wine, cheese, pâtés. Bill says, "You could spend your whole day hanging around the hotel eating for free." But no, he writes, we immediately headed out, climbed Nob Hill, "so as to get into the S.F. feel of things, then walked a great distance and back to Fisherman's Wharf, through Chinatown, North Beach, etc. One's feet began early to make a statement: This was hard work."

Another personal connection in San Francisco brought an evening out with several Amherst students from the early 1960s: "An excellent evening, much talk about Amherst College which both men wanted to hear about."

This conversation reminds me of a longstanding bone of contention between us. Here's the question: Is there a subject besides Amherst College? Bill is a lifer at this institution, having graduated from the place in 1953. He then spent a few years away, first one at Columbia in an unsuccessful attempt to become a philosopher, then four as an English literature grad student at Harvard, where he and I met. (I was an undergraduate at Radcliffe, and there was this production of *The Mikado*, where I sang the ingenue lead and he was the pianist.) He was then called back (a

ABOVE: *Bill on Sproul Plaza, Berkeley,
California, perhaps promoting animal liberation?*
BELOW: *In Seattle, we visited our friends
Dorothy and Roger Sale.*

phrase on Emily Dickinson's gravestone, with a slightly different meaning) to Amherst at age twenty-five to begin a career that will have encompassed six decades in the fall of 2018. Nothing has ever held his attention and interest as much as news, gossip, complaints and observations about this place, most especially its English department. So any evening where there was "much talk" about Amherst would count as an excellent one for him. It didn't always work that way for me.

From San Francisco, where we learn that we've slept through a minor earthquake, we go to Berkeley, and stroll around the university. At Sproull Plaza, site of the early '60s protests, we find tables full of various student groups. The main emphasis is: Get ready for tomorrow's strike for diversity. But there are also tables for animal rights, antidismemberment, Big Brother/Big Sister groups. After an excellent Middle Eastern lunch, we call our son Mike and learned that Bill's Randall Jarrell book has been savaged in the *Washington Post*. My journal notes, "A very favorable one in *USA Today* doesn't quite right the balance."

Next day we hit some of the cultural spots, museum, symphony hall, then meet up with another former student of Bill's, Amy Rabbino, who is now working in City Hall as one of the city supervisor's assistants. She shows us around the building, where earthquake scaffolding is holding up marble veneers and slabs. She then takes us to the Mission District for a hefty Mexican lunch, cafeteria style—huge burritos, our first ever—wrapped in foil with beer on the side.

At eight, we meet the Alperses at Star's. This is an hour when Bill really doesn't like to eat—too late—so the evening is already off to a slightly tainted start. Then there's the fact that we know—via Roger—that they're separating, but they don't know we know, and we know we're not supposed to. It's a flashy, elegant place, and we have intense two-on-two conversations. Bill is happy to hear that Svetlana liked his Jarrell book, and, as he puts it, "We acted as though the Alperses' marital situation had never been better, and things went off smoothly enough. Nothing like a little bad faith to tide you over difficult situations."

The next day we rent a car, a "feeble Ford Tempo," I write, and head north.

> The Bay Bridge in the sun is all that's promised. Next time we'll visit the park on the other side (west) of the road, and climb the hills for an even better view. Muir Woods, just north of the bridge an amazing preserve of redwoods up and down a twisting, scary

"highway" without shoulders. Here it's damp and primordial, with tourists held onto paved paths to keep from damaging the fragile woods. Other trees include a California bay (?) that sends up multiple shoots when downed. [I include a little sketch]

"Next time," I say. That was twenty-six years ago, and although Bill and I did some more traveling together, there was no return to that spot—and won't be, at least not together, since he has given up long-distance travel. But my "next time" represents the traveler's dream, the fantasy that we will remember that detail and return to San Francisco, to the west side of the bridge for a better view. Think of the much-quoted Frost poem "The Road Not Taken." The poem's narrator arrives at a fork in the road, and has to choose which one to take.

> *Oh, I kept the first for another day!*
> *Yet knowing how way leads on to way,*
> *I doubted if I should ever come back.*

We wind our way up the coast and end up at a Luxury Lodge in Bodega Bay. Bill reminds me that this is the scene of Hitchcock's movie *The Birds*, but happily, no sign of any avian hordes at the moment. The Luxury Lodge, Bill notes in his journal, has a "scenic overlook." He's echoing a phrase from a road-trip poem by our old friend Tom Whitbread as he's driving across country: "Scenic Overlooks Overlooked." They're the great views you missed as you whizzed by:

Afternoon, Blue Ridge parkway, sinuous sloth
Through sloshing fogs, our car sea-serpenting
Past Scenic Vistas, Scenic Overlooks
Overlooked, unseen, passed at no miles per hour.

We don't miss that view, but the next morning on our way east, Bill realizes that he's forgotten the jacket to his suit. Back to Bodega Bay with, as I write, "much gloom from him." He does not like making mistakes, revising plans, doesn't like it when others do. There was an even more embarrassing occasion in England after a visit to the writer Antony Powell some years earlier. This time I was the one who forgot a raincoat. We'd had a fine lunch and plenty of literary conversation and gossip with Powell and his wife, Lady Violet, at their comfortable home in Frome, and were headed to view the stately home at Longleat, about twenty minutes away when we realized my mistake. We had to turn around, waste time, and, worst of all, bother our hosts, who by contrast with our unease seemed quite unperturbed. Bill, I think, has still not forgiven me.

In Sonoma, we visit a winery, where we have what I describe as a "perfunctory tour and tastes of some not-great wine," then proceed to Napa, where we've signed up for a night in Bowen Manor Court. Here's Bill.

> Bowen Manor Court was advertised as rural, elegant, etc. As we discovered it up a dirt road, the reality was somewhat different, a falsely "southern" front to an ordinary house—a promise of luxuriance belied by the old toilet seat resting out behind the gashouse. Anyway, it was a reasonably priced room and the woman standing in for the landlady seemed anxious to please. We could have a little sherry if we wanted it; ice was provided. As for restaurants in town, she confessed that the downtown was a bit "Bohemian," and of course we did not flinch at that prospect. But in fact downtown Napa was empty, tourists and others conspicuous by their absence. We lit upon a Mexican restaurant where, for 26 bucks or so total, we had a splendid dinner. But there is not much to do afterwards in Napa, and even (especially?) on Saturday night, and we headed back to Bowen Manor Court for some reading.

On to heavily touristed Sausalito, described by me as a "fishing village turned to T-shirt capital," where, according to Bill, we have the only "bona fide greasy hamburger of the trip." Then it's back to San Francisco for a final night in the huge St. Francis Hotel, which, my journal notes, has "a motel smell and outside elevators—oof. But lots of towels and shampoo and great views." A final excellent Italian meal on Nob Hill, and we get ready to get back on the train heading south early the next morning.

On this leg of the journey, we encounter one of those themed groups that can—and did—make life miserable for those who aren't part of them. Years earlier we had been stuck with one of these on a British train to York, where a drunken group of loutish footballers found each other intensely and loudly entertaining. This time it was the Spanish Heritage group of Santa Clara. My take on this is brief: "We trade annoyed glances with Aussie and English young pairs across the aisle." Bill is more inspired to turn their antics into comedy.

> This was Testing Day for the committed trainer. The test was in the form of a group of jovial tourists, the Spanish Heritage Society, which joined our coach at Santa Clara. Indeed the train was relatively empty as it left Oakland, but the condition was short-lived. The Heritagers were beginning an 18-day roustabout,

taking them across the U.S. by train and bus, to St.
Louis, Memphis, Washington, Disney World, New
Orleans and other prime spots. They were people (to
improvise on a Jarrell locution) who made you dis-
believe in the existence, say, of Wordsworth. They
chattered and honked and screamed with laughter,
brought off brilliant sexual innuendos, many of them
at the expense of one Julio, a leading light, evidently.
They pointed out things in the landscape to each
other, loudly; they told returning members who had
been off exploring other coaches what had happened
in their absence. Everything was a lark! I identified
with the surly Australian girl across the aisle who kept
casting looks back at them. But they were not to be
dealt with through looks. Eventually the view out the
window became interesting enough to divert one's
attention from the Spaniards. I had the worst lunch
of the trip, in the "lounge," a tuna fish thing of some
dubious sort. [We got into L.A. late, but in time to get
on the cars to Flagstaff, our next target.] An important compensation: dinner was served, though late,
and the roast beef catch-of-the-day was, surprisingly,
short ribs. Excellent, after which fell heavily into bed;
or rather not so much a bed as a rather firm board-like
structure not meant for slumbering.

Next stop, Flagstaff, Arizona, and a bus to the Grand

Canyon. Bill is not a happy camper. "I may have been a little whiny or mournful as we pulled into Flagstaff in a brisk
snowstorm," he writes. "How could one view the Canyon
in such terms?" Meanwhile, I am making some different
observations.

A chilly, nervous start to our day at the Grand
Canyon. The station in Flagstaff had few mod cons—
only one toilet and a vending machine with candy
bars—all this at 6:50 a.m. We ate grapes and nuts [I try
always to have snack foods available] and waited for the
Nava-Hopi bus (get it?). Went out in the mushy snow
to try to find coffee and newspapers, just got wet feet.
Got out my silk underwear and layered up.

The canyon lived up to its publicity. Only about
20 people on our bus, a well-versed bus driver com-
mented on the geology, landscape, history, and told
mother-in-law jokes. (I tried to buy jewelry but failed
at our stops.)

The spirit of 19th century conservationism pervades
the main Grand Canyon Village, a fine old rustic hotel,
could be Adirondacks or White Mountains, handsome, restrained landscaping. And across the way,
nature roars away. We gape at various spots, move
on, gape some more. Finally a big buffet lunch
just before the Italian and Japanese tours arrive.

A movie—IMAX—on the way back. See nature, then
see the art to tell you about what you saw. Then the
world's most expensive McDonald's and a sleepy ride
back into snow. My sharp words at lunch seem to have
brought Bill back from the land of gloomy travelers.

Bill's gloom reminds me of the story of the travels of
some friends of ours with the famous/infamous music
critic Bernard Haggin. The friends had been touring in
Italy, driving around and enjoying various sites, while Haggin had done nothing but complain and make things difficult. At a certain point, finding herself at the end of her
patience, one of them turned to him and said: "Bernard,
we have four more days on this trip. Let's try to make them
bearable, and then we never have to see each other again."

After the Grand Canyon, my journal peters out, but Bill
sturdily continues, through Saint Louis, where we spend
a couple of nights with a hospitable newspaper friend of
mine. Then we're back onto the train, Chicago next, and
eventually Springfield. On this last leg, Bill's spirits lift as he
encounters a more familiar if less spectacular landscape.

Sunday, April 28, 1990
    I woke around 5, peered out the window for a
long time, eventually, an hour or so later, found we

were stopped outside Buffalo. That, for some reason, pleased me. To be in New York State yet once more. We had a tremendous breakfast (especially good, I thought) seated across from an oldish black woman who turned out to be a fount of eloquence on all subjects. Riding across New York State was fine, good views of farmland, woodland, and the Mohawk River. I had never ridden across it by train, by day. At Albany we debarked briefly; they unhooked the cars to New York City, and eventually we headed home, not before noting that the Celtics had humiliated the Knicks the previous day (a hint of the future, I so wrongly thought). The route through Massachusetts is especially interesting, vivid scenery through Hinsdale, Chester, etc., up the mountain, along the dam and suddenly you're past Westfield and chugging into West Springfield. There to be met by David, our circle completed.

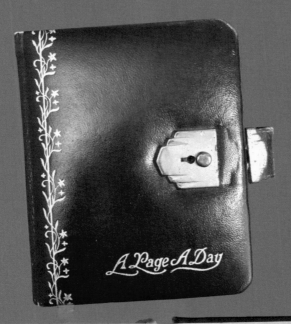

#5 of Music + Art (especially the Art part)

OCTOBER 24 1951

School - Nothing exciting.
We didn't have hockey so we
had basketball instead. I'm
really terrifically out of
condition. Afterwards Beedy
& I walked home. Both Tom &
Johnny walked Mary home.
Poor gal! Bag says that John
is going to ask me to her party.
Hope so, I wish I could straighten
out that mixup with him. God
only knows why I had to go
and tell Polly and Fran that I
don't particularly like him. The
only way you can be sure to
keep a secret anytime is not
to tell anybody! nothing but
nothing! I've got to write
Puttney so I guess I will -

OCTOBER 25

I'm in a very strange mood tonite.
We got our marks today & I have
a 95 average. I'm really not as
glad as I should be because I feel
sort of like a social outcast. It's
queer because if you have low marks
you're more like one of the gang
but getting high ones sort of puts
you in a class by yourself. Very strong
Fran is having loads of trouble with
Willie. Poor frustrated girl. She's much
too good for him. I wish she'd real-
ize that all he's doing is getting
her a bad reputation. I'm going to
the S.H.S. game tomorrow. Should be fun!
I wish I could see or hear from Kenny
again. He's so different from any other
boy I ever met. I'd better not get too
anxious though cuz the same thing
always happens when I do! Just have to
wait til next summer. Rah rah!

My childhood diary, turquoise ink, teenage angst.

Juvenilia

MY EARLIEST WRITINGS about travel, as well as anything else—my childhood diary entries, my adolescent notations, look and sound now like messages not just from another time but from another planet. To me they are fascinating despite the fact that they're often just plain banal; they're innocent yet at the same time somehow stale. They're mine, but they feel derived, a parody of what I might have thought I should be writing. How does a kid know what to record? What to express? How to express it? When, I wonder, did I begin to find what emerged as "my" voice? Or are all those earlier voices equally mine?

As a child I was given a small brown leather-bound diary with a brass clasp on a strap. The gilt-edged pages are narrowly blue-lined and there is a date, but no day or year at the top, so you could use the book for any year. The front pages include a horoscope, a list of birthstones, wedding anniversaries, dates for Easter from 1930 to 1960, population of principal cities of the U.S., brief descriptions of the

Seven Wonders of the Ancient World, some rules for spell-
ing, and weights and measures, including some true obscu-
rities—troy weight, apothecaries' weight and mariners'
measure. At the bottom of that page, you can learn that 12
inches equals 1 foot and 3 miles equals 1 league. The book
has a white ribbon to mark your place, stained with real
ink from the fountain pens I used. The tiny key that came
with it is long lost and was never of much use anyway. (I'm
certain of this because I remember using a hairpin to break
into my sister's diary, which had much the same kind of
key.) Entwined gilt flowers run up the left-hand side of the
cover, and flowing gold letters announce "A Page A Day."
Those were the instructions and limitations: every day
a page, no more, no less. A mostly dutiful child, I didn't
always write a full page, but I never exceeded one. On the
other hand I never kept it up for long, which I believe is
the experience of many hopeful diarists. I must have been
given the little book for Christmas in 1946, when I was ten,
because it begins on Wednesday, January 1, 1947. Here is
what I recorded: "Not much happened. The Angelonies
came and so did some other friends of Mommy's. I almost
got sick from smoke. Also it snowed. Yippee!"

Next day, I wrote: "I was going to go to the Engelhardts
over night and see television but I got sick! (Grrrr!!!!!)

In the morning I had a snowball fight with Dodo."

Someone, probably my father, must have said: Here's a diary, with dates and lines to write on, or, some years later, a nice book with blank pages. Write down what you did every day. Try to describe what you were thinking. Maybe make some sketches of what you saw. Be as honest as you can. It was something he believed in, though it was also something neither he nor my mother did. Both of them were letter writers with extensive correspondences throughout their lives. With letters, you know who your audience is. You can be funny or serious, conventional or outrageous, soothing or challenging, as the situation or person demands. But writing for yourself is another beast entirely. Hello, who's out there? Am I looking into the mirror? Into the future? Imagining myself reading this a few decades on? Imagining others reading this after my own final absence?

NOT MUCH IS TO BE LEARNED from my entries in 1947, although a few details emerge: People still smoked—a lot. And only one person I knew at that time—Julia Engelhardt—had a television set. Her father was an engineer, and it was a quite an exciting revelation for those of us who had grown up with our ears pressed to the radio, that tiny screen, about six inches across, with its black-and-white images embedded in a large piece of furniture. Those 1947 entries fade out quickly, after just a few days. I must have lost interest in recording my life. I find only one more, on November 29: "Dodo and Mommy went to the opera. Daddy and I stayed at home." That must have seemed newsworthy enough to record, but it's tantalizingly lacking in detail. What did Daddy and I do? What did we eat? He did not cook, so either my mother prepared something or perhaps we went out. Did we play one of the card games at which he always beat me? We'll never know.

Later entries appear in 1949 and again in 1951. I am twelve and then fourteen. The handwriting goes from uncertain to prim, with smudged blue fountain pen ink and some pencil in the early entries, then, at fourteen, a very precise printing in a bright turquoise ink with occasional sketches and comments in the margins as I reach full-blown adolescence. At this point there are lots of after-school activities, sports and piano and dancing lessons, hanging out with my girlfriends, mooning over boys, commenting on people's behavior, worrying about what goes into being popular, worrying about being too noticeably successful in school. Here's an entry from October 1951, when I am in tenth grade: "I'm in a very strange mood tonite. We got our marks today and I have a 95 average. I'm really not as glad as I should be because I feel sort of like a social outcast. It's queer because if you have low marks you're more like one of the gang." Sad but true, especially for girls, in my experience. Don't be too smart; better to be one of the gang. I kept my head down after that, but not too much. I managed to get into Radcliffe, where I found myself among people much, much smarter than me, and who were prepared to show it.

Other details bring back aspects of a lost time. About a dozen pages of the diary in 1949, the year I was twelve to thirteen, have just the word "sick" scrawled across them. I certainly spent most or all of that time in bed, a historic fact worth mentioning, since mandatory bed rest soon went out of fashion. By the time our own children were young, that strategy was found to be both unnecessary and debilitating. On the other hand, it was during those times of enforced quiet that I learned to knit, made my way through many books, and listened to lots of radio soap operas. Those were the days before antibiotics, so staying home in bed was one of the only treatments. Both my sister and I contracted the usual series of children's diseases—measles, mumps, chicken pox. I even had scarlet fever at age four, which meant there was a quarantine; my sister had to stay with another family, and we had to get rid of most of my toys.

Later journals reflect a growing interest in getting things down right. I kept one in the summer of 1953 in a severe black soft-covered leatherette book with the word Record on the cover. Pages are numbered and lined, but there are no dates or horoscopes or other useful information. It is truly a blank book. That year I was sixteen and had just finished my junior year in high school. I was spending the summer with a family in France, along with a group of American teenagers, under the auspices of the Experiment in International Living. There, I came to admire the large, hospitable family that I was staying with and tried hard to fit into the life of a small French town. "Be flexible" was one of the Experiment slogans. The other was "Expect the unexpected." Not bad advice for anyone traveling anywhere at any time of life. Maybe the advice extends to life in general. In any case I took it seriously.

That summer, according to my journal, I spent lots of time writing letters home to my high school boyfriend, my parents, and a couple of girlfriends who were working as camp counselors. On a camping trip of our own, my group traveled to the south of France, taking our bikes on trains, then sleeping in tents at various sites. This mainly worked well, although some trouble arose as it became obvious that the French kids were doing most of the work. We tried to improve things by doing more of the chores, including shopping and cooking, making the effort not to be seen as spoiled, ugly Americans. On July 20, I wrote about the preparation of a meal:

> After much discussion we decided on cauliflower with cheese sauce with ham in it. Lynne, Dave I and II [there were two Davids in the group], Tommy and I went into Avignon. Found out that cauliflower was out of season so bought squash instead. Tommy being very unpleasant per usual. He manages to find something to complain about no matter what happens. Really had lots of cooperation on the dinner. I felt as if all future Franco-American relationship hinged on the thing. The squash turned out pretty good and the cheese sauce didn't exactly sauce but was very good anyway. I was so nervous about the whole business cuz the French are just convinced we're completely good-for-nothing.

A later memorable disaster involved my solo cooking. I had offered to make a noodle dish, and in my inexperience, started by dumping the uncooked noodles into cold

water and heating them up. The result was an inedible
noodle paste. We must have improvised something else
that evening, but it became a standing joke. I was pursued
by "Nouilles à l'eau froide" for the rest of the summer.

A COUPLE OF YEARS LATER, IN 1955, after my fresh-
man year in college I traveled first with my parents in Italy,
then studied German and other less official adolescent
subjects at a summer school in Austria. Traveling with my
parents was a relatively new experience. During my childhood, from age six on, I had spent my summers in a series
of camps while they had their vacations on their own. So
they were used to having that time to themselves and I was
used to having the company of my peers. In my journal
from the Italian tour, I register lots of art seen in museums
and churches. I'd had a good art history course my fresh-
man year and was pleased now to see many of the works I'd
studied from slides in person, as it were. But I also chafed
at having to deal with my mother, who I seemed always to
be fighting with and who I found impossibly unreasonable.
She surely must have felt the same about me.

When I was on my own, or at least away from my parents that summer, I kept careful lists of my expenditures.
I must have had a packet of traveler's checks on which I

Summer 1953, I sail for France with the Experiment in International Living. The handsome young man remains nameless. The glamorous postcard of the ship bears no resemblance to the grubby vessel I remember.

could draw, in those distant days before ATMs. On 7/24, for instance, I paid tuition at the summer school of $140. The same day I had a café au lait for 5.50 (this must be in Austrian schillings; Austria was very inexpensive in the postwar period. My research tells me that that was a 25-cent cup of coffee). On a trip to Vienna a few weeks later, I bought fruit for 2 schillings, spent 8 on cigarettes, 6 on toothpaste.

By comparison with my only sporadic journal keeping, the teenaged Bill kept much more careful daily records of both his "ordinary" and special days. These comprise three separate spiral-bound, black daybooks between 1948 and 1950, the end of high school into early college. He kept track not only of daily events, but also amassed a list of movies he'd seen and money he'd earned playing in a band during his high school years. On January 5, 1948 (a school night, I note), he had a piano lesson after school, then after supper went to the movies: "Saw 'Wild Harvest' with Ladd, Foster, Nolan, & Lamour. Also 'Heartaches.' Walked home with Boyd Frost. Listened to the radio and went to bed about 11:00." In addition, he kept track of the local sports teams, one of which he was on, playing for his church, All Saints Episcopal. Statistics about these games appear as carefully pasted-in clippings from the paper, sometimes corrected by him in ink. On the previous

We camped in the south of France during my summer there.

Saturday, January 3, for instance, his team played the Sarah Jane Johnson Methodist Church's team. Young Pritchard, right forward, scored five field goals and one foul shot for a total of 11 points. His team won, 43–36.

Comparing the styles and content of Bill's and my diaries presents some interesting contrasts. Both of us were busy kids, high achievers academically with many outside interests and activities—music, sports, friends, movies, even at times books read for pleasure. The pages recording Bill's days as a junior in high school are mainly factual: did this, saw that, went to bed at this hour, made this many baskets in our game, got this grade on my math test, had a piano lesson. Mine from about the same time include much of the same sort of information but are far heavier on the emotional content. I was angry, sad, disappointed. Lots of trying to understand my own and other people's behavior. I can't help wondering if this is largely gender related. My observation of my own three sons is that they each amassed great quantities of information about a subject of interest. David became a comics collector and bibliophile; Mike (who now owns a record store) knew all about movies, especially horror and sci-fi; Will learned kings and presidents, then turned to sports and music. I don't remember knowing any girls who were archivists in this particular

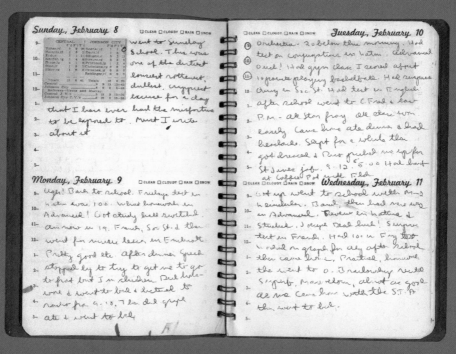

Bill kept meticulously detailed track of his
high school life in two black daybooks.

way. For many boys, it's just the facts, bud, which is not to say they don't have feelings or yearnings, but that they're less likely to articulate them at an early age.

Both Bill and I did some traveling around the time of our junior year in high school. The comparison is amusing and revealing. In late March of 1948, Bill, now fifteen, took one of several trips with his mother to New York City. This was obviously a great release for her from her life as a public school music supervisor. She had done her own graduate work in New York before she was married, and had loved the life of the city. Bill's father, who had minimal interest in travel, didn't join them. Bill and his mother took the train to the city on a Wednesday and returned on Sunday. Both of them went to school the next day. Here is some of what he recorded:

> **Wednesday, March 31**
> **Woke up at 5:15. Didn't know what time it was. Finally had Craig turn on radio** [he shared a room with his younger brother] **& then went back to sleep. Up at 6:30. Ate breakfast, washed dishes and finished packing. We left the station at 8:30. Train was 20 minutes late & we were late all the way to NY. Had dinner on train & when we got to NY took tubes to 34th Street, then taxi to Abby** [hotel]**. Got settled**

Our three sons on a warm Christmas Day in the 1980s.
From left, Mike, David and Will.

in room & then walked over & took 3rd Ave. El to
Bowery & Chinatown. Ate at Panfin [illegible] Rest.
Good. Walked over to Broadway & took bus up to
Radio City. Got in line & saw "I Remember Mama"
with Irene Dunne & Easter Revue. Went to bed but
not to sleep.

Thursday, April 1

Mother didn't sleep well & we almost decided to
change rooms. Ate breakfast over at Taft Grill. Fair.
Went to Museum of Science & Industry which was
very interesting. Mother was tired, so we came back
to the hotel & switched rooms. She lay down & I
went to show. Saw "Adventures of Robin Hood"
with Flynn, Pallette, DeHaviland, Rathbone. Good.
Went to couple of amusement galleries. Came back
to room & rested, we got dressed & ate at Brass Rail
Restaurant. Delicious dinner. Took Lexington Ave.
bus to Hunter College & heard Rubenstein. Superb.
Back on Madison Ave. bus. Walked around Times
Square. Had taffy apple. Bed.

The next days are chronicled in much the same detail,
though there are ways of reading between the lines, if you
know the characters involved. Bill accompanied his
mother to "Jack Wanamaker's," one of the old great

department stores on lower Broadway. I got to know his mother's shopping habits from accompanying her in much later years as she tried to find Christmas presents for our boys or some item or other for herself. She was a dogged and hard-to-satisfy customer. So when Bill writes: Took bus to Jack Wanamaker's & looked & looked around. Finally took the subway . . ." I can detect a bit of exasperation with his mother's habit of lingering. Perhaps this early history accounts for his later determination to avoid shopping of any kind except for food—well, and except for books and records. That evening they saw *Man and Superman*, which Bill describes as "swell." Bill says about the following day: "This was the day." Indeed: Natural History Museum, Hayden Planetarium, Times Square for lunch, Paul Kelly in *Command Decision* ("which I liked immensely"). After the movie, they went to the NBC studios, where a friend "pulled strings," so were able to hear Toscanini conduct the NBC Symphony. Not surprisingly, in the middle of these event-filled days, the young man dozed through most of the concert, a fact that has embarrassed him acutely in later life. Next was dinner at Kean's Chop House ("Delicious") and finally "Wangled way into 'It Pays to Be Ignorant,' " a famous comedy quiz show. The next day, Sunday, "most dreariest of days," they went to church at

St. Thomas, rode the bus up through Harlem and past the
Polo Grounds and Yankee Stadium. "Ate last meal at L'Abbey
& it stank." They took the tube to Hoboken and the train
home. School the next day.

As the diaries continue over the next years, he begins to
include some evidence of interest in girls and an increasing
willingness to express his reactions to people and things in
greater detail—in more than monosyllables. A few years
later, in June of 1951, the summer after his sophomore
year, he traveled with a group of college-age musicians
from Amherst and elsewhere, the small band I mentioned
earlier that was hired to play for the American troops in
Europe. A single page of a diary from that time is stuck
inside one of his other journals. The voice is increasing in
sophistication and breezy humor as he gets his first taste
of liberation from both home and college. He registers
the last day on the steamer where he'd been assigned to
play cocktail piano. His friend Bill Youngren would be the
jazz pianist when they got to Europe. Bill (Pritchard) was
enjoying and suffering with a girl named Ann, to whom
he had to say goodbye as they left the boat. He describes
the experience as "a fairly meaningful one for me. At least
I've had her constantly on my mind—but that's nothing
too new." Then, as he steps off the boat that had been his

home base for a week, he has the odd, slightly mind-altering experience familiar to travelers, of finding themselves abruptly in another place. "Suddenly," he writes "here was Europe & Holland." After checking in to a hotel, having a drink at a sidewalk café, and taking a nap, he has a great meal and a fine fruit sundae. After which he declares, with tongue firmly in cheek: "I like the Dutch—they are clean and happy." A further entry looks like this:

> July 10—We left the Arcade Hotel for Amsterdam. The town was a small gas. We visited the Rijks Museum (art) & just walked around looking at things. Bought a N.Y. Tribune! We had a fine elegant meal—hors d'oeuvres, soup, steak, etc., decent coffee & a cigar. It was about the ultimate in luxurious living. The trainride back to Rotterdam knocked me out at one point, quiet cows grazing on a Dutch meadow at dusk. Passed through customs after taking a train to the HOOK. Had a beer & cheese sandwich on the boat [crossing the Channel] & then sacked.

A few days later the boys in the band are in London. Bill is running down the checklist of important tourist stops, articulating the traveler's eternal hope:

I saw quite a bit of "musts" including Dr. Johnson's hangout, the Old Curiosity Shop & the Tower of London. Boatride back up the Thames & ate in the hotel. Saw Laurence Olivier and Vivien Leigh in "Antony & Cleopatra." It was a real gas—a marvelous production. I hope I'm making enuf out of this trip.

At the bottom of a sheet of onionskin paper, in his tiny, hard-to-read handwriting, is an entry made several months later, New Year's Day, 1952. He is nineteen. It presages a great deal of his later life. I find it quite moving.

My annual New Year's message. This year I have tried to become more of an intellectual—literature, philos, music, etc. I cast off Christianity for better or for worse. I saw a piece of the world & it was impressive & a telling experience. I fell in love—I thought—with Ann Rademacher & had interesting times with Barb, Bev, Marilyn, Kate & Biji. I think I want to be a teacher.

Resolutions—I don't know—to be more self-reliant than ever, to read, read, read & think—to go back to Europe if possible—to see Ann once again—HAPPY N. YEAR.

Wednesday Aug. 24 - Felt weak & sickly. Listened to some jazz at the radio station. Slept much, ate little & played at the officers club at nite. Met Bart Connolly & other people. The band played awfully well at times. Felt better in evening.

Thurs. Aug 25 - Another complete waste. We thought we had a plane but it was not true. So I turned over $173 to J. M Bucky & he & the SARGE. who took off. We viewed part of "Bedtime for Bonjo" & then sacked in early. Some gassed engineers sleeping with us.

Fri Aug 25 - Caught the 8:00 plane & flew along Morocco, Algeria & across the med to Sardinia & landed at Teronto. Had spaghetti & wine & took off for Naples where after we had pizza & wine I am sailing with Bob.

We now have 11 days left of this great long summer. Can't think of anything lucid or philosophical to venture so we'll let it go with that truth alone.

SAT- Aug 26- See Naples & drop dead! We did & feel like doing so. Kibe & bus whistle drove us out & we saw Pompeii then after a great strain we finally got on the train to Rome & felt better after some beer. Registered at the San Remo. So we're in Rome!

Sun 27 - Took bus tours of Ancient & Modern Rome & saw the Forum, Colisseum & many other passes. Great hotel meal — not bad. Saw Symphony concert - Tschaik 4th & Wagner Tristan.

JAN 1- DEC 31 - 1951-2

My annual New Year message. This year I have tried to become more of an intellectual - literature, philo, music etc. I cast off Christianity for better or for worse. I saw a slice of the world & it was an impressive & a telling experience. I fell in love - I thought - with Ann Parkenham & had interesting times with Bart, Pew, Manley, Hate & Biji. I think I want to be a teacher.

RESolutions -- I don't know -- to be more self - reliant than ever, to read, read, read, & think -- to go back to Europe if possible - to see Ann once again -- HAPPY N. Year

Bill wrote a New Year's letter to himself in 1953.

*Bill poses in Italian hat and American topcoat
on a chilly day in Orvieto, 1964.*

Sabbaticals

S ABBATICALS. We had three of them abroad, the first in Rome in 1963–64 with two sons, the elder three years old, the younger eight months; the second in London in 1968–69 with three sons, ages eight, five and three; and the final in London, 1973–74, the three sons now thirteen, ten and eight. I find only a few pages of journals from those times away. It seems that letters took up much of our writing energy.

Sabbatical leaves, when taken away from home with a family, are a special subset of travel. You are a visitor, a traveler, yet you are also a resident. You feel an obligation to take in the sights and the sites, yet you are also establishing a regular domestic routine of school, grocery shopping, meals, piano lessons, and birthday parties, along with a social life with dinner parties and evenings out in restaurants with new acquaintances as well as having friends and relatives from the U.S. arrive on visits. It's supposed to be a great and rich experience. In many ways it was that, but not all of it positive for me. The years in London were many magnitudes better than that first year away in Rome, where, at age twenty-six, I tried to be a supermom. My Italian was pretty good, functional at least, and I learned to navigate the city in our car, a gray Mercury Comet, which had come with us on the ship ($350 round trip). But I was navigating to the laundromat, the market, the nursery school, and the pediatrician, not to the Borghese Gallery and the Sistine Chapel. Bill spent more time exploring the city's ancient monuments, discovering the pleasures of art for himself. He had a nonresident fellowship at the American Academy, with a desk where he could work on his book on the British writer and painter Wyndham Lewis, and where we had the privilege of going for some amazingly bad meals. There was some travel that year for Bill and me, once we found babysitters who could stay with the two boys in Rome for a few days at a time. Later, during our two sabbatical years in London, we did some of the same sort of brief trips as a couple, plus some travel with all five of us, but we never did the major cross-country or cross-continent tours that some families seem to manage. *J'y suis, j'y reste* seemed like a pretty good motto.

Four years after the Roman experience, in 1968–69, although Bill quickly settled into a good relationship with London's literary crowd, a few pages from a journal I briefly kept that year show a pretty high level of restlessness on my part. Despite a number of cultural activities—concerts, visits to museums and historic sites—I never found a satisfactory place of my own. I was enjoying singing with the London Symphony Chorus, which met once a week and which performed several times with the symphony, but my main job description was housekeeper, mom and wife. I enjoyed meeting and entertaining the new group of witty, talented literary people, some of whom were asking Bill to write for their publications, but without outside work of my own or the network of friends I depended on at home, I had a hard time feeling grounded. Upon returning to Amherst in the fall of 1969, I was invited by a good friend to attend a meeting of the newly budding women's liberation movement. I wasn't so sure about its goals or its description of women as an oppressed group, but I went. If I went to scoff, I stayed to pray, and the small support group that I joined became an important part of my life. I think of that moment as a turning point in how I saw and see the world. It did not make things easier between Bill and me, but that's a different story.

My brief London journal begins in September 1968, with a description of a concert by the celebrated baritone Dietrich Fischer-Dieskau at the Royal Festival Hall. I note:

"F.-D. sang Goethe poems set to music by various people—
Beethoven, Schubert, Schumann, Brahms, but also others
too silly to remember. Not a very satisfying program
musically, but he is a great performer—big, young, unfalter-
ing, magnetic. I'd like to hear him sing some good music."
The next day I describe a visit to the central police station,
"where I sat for an hour waiting to be allowed to be an
alien." (As temporary residents, we had to register to be
sure we weren't going to be looking for work that would
deprive real Brits of jobs.) Afterward on that day, lots of
walking and looking, concluding with the observation
that London is "very grand indeed. It seems capable of
caring for most human needs. It's not menacing, yet not
tame either." A couple of months later, I am contending
with the visit of Bill's mother, who has arrived to join us
for Christmas. Marion Pritchard was a strong, determined
woman, by then a widow for nearly a decade, and, at age
sixty-seven, still supervising music in the public schools.
Although I came to admire and eventually love this woman,
in 1968 I was thirty-two and struggling to keep my emotional
head above water. How could I conduct my life when she
was around? I asked. Here's what I wrote:

> It seems to be not much better here than at home.
> I find myself taking needlessly rigid positions and

Sabbatical scenes. ABOVE: *Playing cards
with David, Rome, 1964.* BELOW: *Our cabin on
the* Statendam, *departing for London, 1968.*

tones of voice. When asked would I like to come to
Harrod's and just "look around" tomorrow (here yesterday by plane, she's been in and around stores all
day today). No, say I, I don't like to go to department
stores unless I'm looking for something in particular.
A feebly veiled half truth, since about the only excuse
I need to waste a morning in one of those places is to
be vaguely "looking for something." But not with her,
evidently. All my good intentions to act like a grownup
person and be charitable and generous—bar loving,
that's just not there—disappear, melt, dissolve into a
dew at the sound of her voice. The only solution has
been, still seems to be, to keep my hands and feet as
busy as possible, so the devil won't find my tongue
too readily available. Tonight's LSO chorus rehearsal
was a godsend. I went striding off on my own.

AFTER THE THIRD SABBATICAL, London 1973–74, I de-
clared that I was done with that form of experience. I had
landed my first job as a more or less regular part-time
teacher in 1964, just after we returned from our first sabbatical in Rome. A few weeks after accepting that job, I
discovered I was pregnant yet again. A surprise, which
turned out to be our fine third son. The third sabbatical
had been by far the easiest, since I had now become accus-
tomed to setting up house in a foreign city. But I was not

ABOVE: *David, age 3, reads the paper, with the Castel Sant'Angelo behind him, 1963.*
BELOW: *Grandmother Marion Pritchard with David, left, and Mike. London, 1968.*

being granted sabbaticals of my own. Each time we left, it had meant giving up a job, then searching for a new one when I returned. I felt I needed to get serious about work. I had gone back to school, acquired another teaching credential, and then a master's degree in education, and I'd been working in several local public schools tutoring kids with learning disabilities. After the state's special education law changed in 1972, I was told I'd have to take more education courses. I'd had more than enough of those, and so decided to look for other work. I volunteered at a local public TV station, then did some reporting for a weekly paper. In 1977, I started my first job as an obituary writer at the *Daily Hampshire Gazette* in Northampton, a newspaper where I found my footing as a journalist. I never regretted it, and there were no more sabbaticals away from home.

Looking back from my current status as a certifiably old person, it's entertaining and illuminating to reread the letters we got from our friends during the years we were away. Amherst College, where Bill taught, was a tight, smug little entity. Although there were several other academic institutions in the area, not to mention an area full of people in other walks of life, our social lives revolved around the college and even more tightly around the English department, with a few additions from political science and art history. We were truly provincial—tribal, even. It was a time when alcohol flowed freely at parties, people argued loudly and passionately, and everyone smoked. Not everyone behaved as they should have.

The letters I have saved from those years we were away read like fiction. In fact, some of the life of the Amherst College English department made its way into published fiction. In her 1962 novel *Love and Friendship*, Alison Lurie, who had lived in Amherst as the wife of a young member of the college's English department—a faculty wife, as the designation then went—painted an ironic and entertaining picture of academic life, including a thinly veiled description of a famous/infamous introductory writing course, and an account of a young faculty wife's illicit affair. Here is a letter from a semidetached observer in the book, a visiting writer, describing a party:

> This is a real little miniature universe—by which I don't mean The Universe in miniature. Though some of the more intellectual professors like to think so privately, and the less intellectual say so publicly, Convers [the name of the college] is not a microcosm of the world . . . it is a botanical or zoological garden, where each flower has its cage, each beast or bird its

metal identification tag. When I first turned up every-
one was frightened and nervous of me, but now that
I have my label and show signs of staying quietly put,
I am just one of the exhibits, along with The Janitor
Who Drinks and Bad Oswald McBear.

The latter was greatly in evidence Saturday night,
booming out his boorish bon mots, laughing his
laugh. The only person who managed to pay him
absolutely no attention was his wife Kittie. She just
sat quietly all evening in a corner of the sofa, her tiny
feet crossed, like a good little gray-haired schoolgirl,
letting out little Miaows at the gossip which one or
the other faculty wife was continually telling her. Yet
she has a sharp look.

THE LETTERS WE RECEIVED from our friends seem to
me at least as amusing. Here is a sample. Most of the parti-
cipants have departed from this earth.

The Kennicks had a "mixed" Christmas party (i.e.,
there was a person or two from the University, even
an exchange teacher from Heidelberg who had a little
more grace than most of his ilk), and of course the
Heaths did it up for Roger. (Armour, late and in his
cups, told me to stop smoking in my classroom, told
me it was an order, and Frank said he did not like

seeing people give orders to other people, whereupon
Armour asked Frank what was "bugging" him, whereupon Frank, who knew perfectly well that Armour
meant that Frank had been "bugging" <u>him</u>, argued for
several hours that The Place was bugging him, whereupon Armour wanted still to know what was bugging Frank, until Mary [the letter writer's wife] told
both Armour and Frank to "shut up," meaning especially Frank at that moment, whereupon everyone,
especially Frank and Armour fell to praising Mary's
Olympian wisdom, whereupon Roger said something
nice to Frank and retired to the kitchen with Mel [the
hostess].) Roger (who stayed here) and I went to bed
at 5:30—at 10:00 I let my freshmen go, but somehow
I taught fifty minutes worth of *Middlemarch* though
I can't remember a word I said. . . . Roger had dinner here with the Craigs before the party and there
were a lot of dirty jokes and a great deal of Roger's
hand on Peggy's thigh—more out of a slightly hys-
terical, excessively nostalgic convention than anything
else, I think, though I caught a fleeting, unguarded,
but most penetrating expression on Armour's [Peggy's
husband's] face when Roger and Peggy were snuggling
that made me think that if I were Edmund Spenser I
might be able to describe a character called Jealousy (or
maybe it was Envy—I'm never quite clear about those
two words). But it is true that Roger is in good shape.

Many of the letters take this witty, ironic tone. Our friend
Mel Heath was particularly skilled at this. She was, in fact,
a fine writer of fiction. Here is her account of the same
event.

We gave the party this time, Camerons gave the bed,
and Coles rushed around warning all of us not to
keep Roger up too late as he was very tired as though
Roger were ever as tired as anybody else anyway. That
sentence didn't quite make it. We had the Honor
Guard plus Kennicks, DeMotts, Mishkins, Chametz-
kies, yes really. Bairds said yes, then no as usual. So
what to eat? Welsh Rarebit Rabbit, Mrs. Townsend
and I had long discussion about what is PROPER
pronunciation which I of course won though she may
not know it. But it would not jell until Frank poured
half a bottle of whiskey in it; it turned then to a sort
of molded cheese in a whiskey aspic, quite novel actually. Mrs. Mishkin put on her coat to go home as she
took it off to arrive and left Henry [her husband] to
the tender mercies of Peggy who accused him of pat-
ting Mrs. Alexander's bottom? Yes, I think that's the
way it went. Meanwhile someone spilled a large bag
of garbage and Peggy made Henry pick it up and Ben
had a quiet polite public chat with Armour and the
same with Roger and Mrs. Coles pregnantly had to

have air and Mrs. Romer had to be got because Bob [her husband] stayed late at the lab but her escort was Bill Heath because Roger was engaged by Ben I think at that point. Bill Kennick kept saying he was drunk. He wasn't. Britt spent an hour stirring the Rare Babbit, in a huff. Alan [Britt's husband] adores Mrs. Townsend sort of. Anne Chametzky said she'd never been to a party with less sex. Oh dear and all we've got in Amherst was there practically. . . . Frank and Jack and Bill quietly rowed about why the Kennicks don't invite the Lathams to their Xmas Party until five-thirty. . . . Mrs. Miller came next day and I could hear her going around the house ohmying to herself as she discovered half drunk drinks all over the place and ashes and mess and depravity. Roger left on the five plane—I went along with Mr. Coles to say goodby but Mr. Coles has a Thing about not seeing planes off the ground so I was rushed away before he actually left but it was all terribly romantic, the field was all lit up for miles and the engines gunned or whatever and a gorgeous sunset and twinkling stars and a new moon, what a movie.

Bill and I just shared a cigaret, fighting over the last puff. Days of wine and roses.

So that was the news from the home front. A few years later I was writing obituaries for the *Daily Hampshire Gazette,* with encouragement to write feature articles on the side. I learned the basics of news writing—who, what, where, when—and then had some very good help from the features editor, who taught me how to ask not only those questions, but also the next round of questions, and how to look for a good story. I had to learn to lose the ironic tone when writing newspaper features. It was a very good education for me, a sort of editorial cold shower. I was now both anchored in a challenging form of work and free to do a different kind of travel.

Bill and me at Stonehenge, 1969.

We made a trip around New England in the late '80s and rode on a friend's boat off the coast of Maine.

Travels à Deux

IN THE EARLY 1980S, when our sabbaticals away from home were over, I was working at the newspaper, and our three sons were pretty much on their own, Bill and I fell into a pattern of doing some fairly serious traveling more or less every other summer. His academic summer vacations were long, more than three months; mine, once I started work at the newspaper, were much shorter—two weeks off at first, then after a few years, three weeks. But it was enough, plenty of time for the sort of traveling we wanted to do. The train trip to the West Coast was one of those trips, but there also were several returns to Europe. We were never especially adventurous in our plans, no Kilimanjaro, no whitewater rapids. First off, Italy needed to be rehabilitated for me. My time there as a young wife and mother had been so difficult that I had truly not, in the words of our annoying friend, "known where I was." We returned for the first time in 1982, almost twenty years after our sabbatical year in Rome. Our subsequent travels focused on art, architecture, landscape, visits to friends, and visits to places with literary resonance—these mostly in Britain. Later, as I tried to learn more about my family's history, we traveled—sometimes together, sometimes me on my own or in other company—to Central Europe and France. Eventually Bill dropped out of the travel routine. Meanwhile, I kept on visiting our kids on the West Coast twice a year, along with a few trips with others—a walking tour in Sicily with my sister (my only group travel so far) and a trip to several Greek islands with her and her husband. I still find travel exhilarating, even when it involves layovers in O'Hare or Minneapolis en route to Oregon.

But in 1982, as we headed once again to Italy, this time just the two of us and for only two weeks, there was no hint yet of Bill's back trouble, and he was an ambitious tourist, eager to educate himself further. He wrote an article for our local newspaper's magazine section titled "A Guidebook Odyssey," and I contributed a companion piece.

My piece appeared in tandem with his more prominent one, but I will quote from it here first, partly to anticipate some of his themes—and maybe partly, in a spirit of marital competition, to get my oar in ahead of his. I wrote that marriage is said to be a partnership, and that the pleasures and pains of such a partnership are most noticeable on a

Traveling By The Book
with William H. Pritchard

Bill, shown here in Venice in 1982,
wrote about guidebooks for our local paper.

traveling vacation. For weeks before our departure, our
living room had been littered with books about Italy—
art books, history books, maps and guidebooks. Was I,
I wondered, going to be able to live up to the itinerary
being assembled here?

Well, yes and no, it turned out. My strength is
definitely not in the guidebook department (although
I like to read them *after* I've been somewhere), but I
love to look at things, to discover my own unexpected
"sights," and I love to listen and talk. I am an enthu-
siastic amateur photographer and a lover of foreign
languages. (My love of language has not led me to
know any one of them expertly, but has left me at the
level of the linguistic dilettante in several—somewhat,
I imagine, like being a first grader learning to read.
I am simply delighted at understanding and making
myself understood.)

My husband, on the other hand, would prefer not to
venture into languages in which he doesn't feel expert.
And the combination of our strengths and limitations
turned what might have merely been a series of irrita-
tions into a surprisingly successful venture.

While Bill steered a steady course from monument
to monument, from one great work of art to the
next, I was able to stop him and catch the odd human

I took pictures of doorbells in Florence.

drama—the bride and groom in full regalia stopping
at an ice cream vendor for respite from the Roman
heat. And since I didn't have to worry about the route
we were taking, I could wander off to admire (and
photograph) a wonderful variety of brass doorbells
installed in front of many apartments in Florence.
I wasn't avoiding the masterpieces, it was just that I
didn't have to worry about how to get to them—that
is, unless we got lost or needed help of some other
sort. And that's where my role as linguistic dilettante
came in handy. When a church on an island near
Venice was closed (an all-too-common predicament
for sightseers in Italy), I was able to inquire about taking the boat to the cemetery island of San Michele
where we went instead to visit the graves of Stravin-
sky and Ezra Pound.

But it was not only a combination of happy oppo-
sites. My husband and I do agree on a thing or two.
And two of them are food. From Italian ice cream
cones to seafood marinara, you can hardly go wrong
when you eat in Italy, and we ate well and often. (After
all, you have to keep your strength up for sightseeing.)
One of the most pleasant meals we had was a picnic
lunch in an overgrown park. The food was simple—
fresh mozzarella, fresh salami, fresh bread, black
olives and the most amazing blood oranges. That stop
wasn't in the guidebook.

I view Venice from above.

Meanwhile, the guidebooks that Bill favored for that trip were the *Blue Guides* to Northern Italy and Rome. In the piece he wrote for the magazine, he describes how he saw them, how they were helpful.

I began the process of trying to improve myself as a seer and knower of the sights. These two books were my main equipment to do battle with the scenes revisited or seen for the first time. And indeed the traveler hooked on guidebooks is, without them, like a warrior deprived of his armor. Defenseless, he may just have to stare at the cathedral, the building, the landscape.

Of course there is a fair portion of guilt which accrues to employing such an aid to reflection. You can understand this guilt if you have ever come upon a painting in a museum and almost before looking at the canvas your eyes have darted involuntarily down to the painter's name, the title of the picture and its date of composition. There is nothing really reprehensible about behaving this way; after all, once you get the name (Sandro Botticelli, "Primavera," 1480?) you may relax and begin to look at the picture, muttering things like "So this is the way old Botticelli does it, eh" etc. . . .

Suppose, for example, you want to see Bernini's

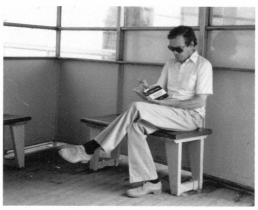

If it wasn't in the guidebook, it probably wasn't worth seeing.

marble elephant with the obelisk on top of it (in
Rome's Piazza Minerva). Instead of heading directly
for the Piazza, if you are a dutiful Blue Guide user,
you will try to hook into one of the planned routes
which includes Piazza Minerva and the elephant as
one of its sights. So you read that "The narrow Via
del Gesu (II, D2) runs N. from the Piazza del Gesu
(p. 43) which unites the Via del Plebiscito with the
Corso Vittorio Emanuele."

After quite a few more sentences, the guide—and the
guided reader, presumably—arrives at the "desired elephant." Sometimes, he notes, there are surprises, such
as finding the building you came to see closed or covered
with scaffolding. And sometimes, he writes, "you may be
so pleased with yourself for having navigated the distance
between objects with a minimum of confusion, that you
can barely concentrate on the object you thought you
came to see."

Here the insidiousness of depending on a guidebook
takes over, at that moment when you wonder whether
really you didn't enjoy getting all the left-right, N.W.-
S.E. business down perfectly a good deal more than
you did the noble edifice it led you to. This is called

the "Oh What a Good Boy (or Girl) Am I" syndrome, and will serve as an example of the pride that goeth before a fall. Yet experiencing it can bring a dash of health and reality to the whole enterprise, reminding you that you *are* different from the guidebook and that you've had sensations, however unworthy, which were not written down or dreamed of in all the guide's comprehensive mastery of things.

Later, in Venice, he puts down his *Blue Guide* in favor of a less strenuous book, *Venice for Pleasure*, by J. G. Links. Links provides him with permission to skip some "great" sights, such as all fifty-six Tintorettos in the Scuola Grande di San Rocco. As Links put it: "It would be unthinkable to visit Venice without seeing them. Never let it be said that I suggested such a thing. I only point out that the stairs are steep, the pictures, though wonderful, profuse, and that they will still be there tomorrow, and indeed on our next visit to Venice." Enough said, says Bill; "This time I took the Linksian, coward's way out." But sometimes Links points the way to a closer look. After urging the traveler to take in the first nineteen rooms of the Accademia in half an hour, he points to a couple of rooms where, he admits, "We are held up badly, first by a stunning St. George by Mantegna, then by some glorious small Giovanni Bellinis and a Piero della Francesca St. Jerome." At this point, Bill writes, "The idea of being 'held up badly' (as in a traffic jam on Route 91 between Hartford and Springfield) is a fine piece of wit when applied to Mantegna and Piero, and makes one look at them more attentively." Links now directs the visitor out of the Accademia and into a café, saying, "We can take no more beauty and fortunately there is little more to take."

At the end of his piece, Bill quotes admiringly from a genuinely indefatigable writer/traveler, Henry James.

> At least half the merit of everything you enjoy must be that it suits you absolutely; but the larger half here is generally that it has suited someone else and that you can never flatter yourself you have discovered it. It has been addressed to some use a million miles out of your range, and has had great adventures before ever condescending to please you.

"The nice thing," Bill concludes, "is that it does so condescend, and that the guidebook, by giving an account of what has 'suited someone else,' challenges us to see if we can enter into the continuity of impressions and pleasure."

But there weren't always guidebooks to help Bill out. In 1991, I planned a trip to Hungary in search of more information about my family, especially my father's Hungarian branch. I started out with my sister, my mother, and my niece. Bill joined me at a later stage in the trip.

My father, who was born in 1895, had died in 1988; paradoxically, perhaps, his absence had freed me to pursue this project. He had written a memoir, at my request, which included plenty of information about his early life, but he had not wanted to go back to Hungary. He feared and hated the Communist regime and felt profoundly uneasy on a single postwar visit. The year after his death, 1989, my sister, my mother and I traveled in Hungary. It was the year the Communists departed, although evidence of their presence was still strong. Two years later, we three headed for the Czech Republic and the small town of Sušice, my mother's hometown. We were joined in Prague by my sister, Dodo's, daughter, Katie, who had been living and teaching English to Hungarians in Budapest after college.

I was continuing to look into my family's past. My initial visit to Hungary in 1989 had sparked what turned into a decades-long effort and resulted eventually in my book *Among Strangers*. After that first trip "back," I had begun to try to learn Hungarian, my father's language, one that had been spoken around us as we grew up, but which my sister and I were not encouraged to learn. It was easier to pick up a little of the German, our mother's language, which was also spoken at home, which was taught in college classrooms, and which I'd encountered from learning to sing lieder. Czech was another story, but we found it possible to function in the Czech Republic with a mixture of English and German. At age eighty-four, our mother, amazingly, still remembered some of her childhood Czech, and so could fill in the gaps when we were really stymied. Although seriously hampered by a bad hip that would soon be replaced, Mother undertook this return to her childhood home with typical energy and determination. She did not seem overcome by emotion, but was mainly pleased and animated by connecting with the past. There were still a few people around who remembered her family, along with some of the same details that she did.

Our mother's family's house in the town square had been converted into a cooperative grocery store, but the family's industry, the manufacture of matches, was still operating. (It has since closed, with all the machinery sent to India, where, it seems, matches are still widely used.) Founded in the nineteenth century by Mother's great-grandfather Bernhard Fürth, the industry had been run by Fürth family members until World War II, when it was taken over first by the Nazis and then after the war by the Communists.

Labels from matchboxes for the wooden matches
manufactured by my mother's family in Bohemia.

In 1991 it was once again privately owned. The managers
greeted our mother cordially, but with what seemed to be
a bit of wariness. Was she, perhaps, going to make moves
to claim ownership of the factory? Many such claims were
being mounted in the postwar, post-Communist era. She
persuaded them, I think, that she had no such intentions,
nor did anyone else in the family. This was purely a sen-
timental journey. We met with them the morning after
we arrived in town, and they toasted us with *becherovka*,
a throat-clearing schnapps. We were then taken on a tour
of the factory buildings, where Mother was delighted to
recognize the machines and lumber piles of her childhood.

We had spent a couple of nights in Prague before going
to Sušice, and we now went on to some straightforward
tourist activities, visiting several charming places before
heading for Bratislava, where we would separate. The three
others headed for Vienna, and I took the train to Budapest,
where I met up with Bill and our son Will at the Gellért
Hotel. Here is how Bill starts his journal of that trip:

To make use of Frost's formulation ["a poem begins
in delight and ends in wisdom"] : This trip was like a
poem inasmuch as it began in anxiety and ended in
a flourishing head cold. In between what was there?

I kept resisting making Statements, even as I made them to myself. Like: I have very little capacity for being interested in all sorts of things outside myself, from farms in Hungary to the history of Amsterdam. More and more the best parts of the tourist's day were ones in which he collapsed for The Serious Nap. Or tucked into one of those European martinis, or delighted in a splendid main course. Much of the time of every day was spent, however, feeling relatively out of control. This is not like reading a poem or writing a review. The words I have in response to some bit of artifact or blot of landscape seem boring and inadequate. The tourist's mind does not feel particularly interesting, or alive, or engaged. Was it always thus, or is it increasing with age? [He was 59.]

Hungary really began very well, making our way to the Gellért where Marietta beamed in the lobby, glad to see us (and vice versa). A splendid hotel, room, lots of English spoken at front desk. In fact the tourist with no Hungarian might be advised to settle in at the Gellért, close to the front desk, where his every want will be provided for. The restaurant that first night was splendid however, The Carpathian, informal and handsomely roomy, a fine looking Hungarian martini followed by excellent wienerschnitzel, then a walk back across the Elizabeth Bridge over the gorgeous Danube, Gellért gleaming to the left.

That was about as good as it got for Bill. Pretty quickly
he settled into his mode of "very little capacity for being
interested in all sorts of things outside myself." And I had
settled into my attitude of very little patience with his
complaints. "Absolutely no pleasure, no lightness of touch,"
I write about him a few days later in my journal. Not long
after, I am swearing never again to do this kind of traveling
with him. I will go alone or with others, I vow. Still, this is
only the beginning of our trip together, and we need to
soldier on, for better or worse. I am on a mission to find
the farm in the eastern part of the country where my
father had lived and managed things for a couple of years.
He had written about it in his memoir. The place had surely
been collectivized under the Communists, but maybe
there was still something to see, I hoped, maybe some people
who remembered the time before the war. Meanwhile, the
difference in Bill's and my ways of approaching new places
was perhaps getting exaggerated. Were we becoming par-
odies of ourselves? I was, as a friend once said—not entirely admiringly—when I produced a Swiss Army knife from
my pocketbook, a regular Girl Scout. I was attempting to
be prepared, expecting the unexpected, keeping my chin
up—perhaps being something of a prig. Bill was—well,
here's a passage from Nathaniel Hawthorne's travel note-

books that Bill quoted admiringly in a review a few years
after that trip:

> If my wits had not been too much congealed, and my
> fingers too numb, I should like to have kept a minute
> journal of my feelings and impressions during the past
> fortnight. It would have shown modern Rome in an
> aspect in which it has never yet been depicted. . . . The
> first freshness of my discomfort has worn off, so that
> I shall never be able to express how I dislike the place,
> and how wretched I have been in it. . . . Cold, narrow
> lanes, between tall, ugly, mean-looking, whitewashed
> houses, sour bread, pavements most uncomfortable to
> the feet, enormous prices for poor living.

Bill then comments on the passage: "Hawthorne's genius
responds most fully to the experience of a new place when
it's felt in every way to be inimical, an assault equally on
the flesh and spirit." Yes indeed. By the time he wrote this
review—of Henry James's travel writings—Bill had begun
to settle firmly into his antitravel mode, nodding happily
when anyone else spoke negatively about a travel experience.
Meanwhile, on we went into the Hungarian countryside,
onto the Great Hungarian Plain, the *puszta.* In *Among
Strangers,* I describe this part of the trip and draw a general

conclusion about Bill from his resistance to my search:

> Unlike me, Bill has had all the roots he has ever need-
> ed or wanted. When I first visited his family in a small
> city in upstate New York, I was amazed to discover
> in what proximity they lived to each other. Amazed
> and, I'll have to admit, appalled. From the backyard
> of his parents' house, you could yell down two houses
> to where his three aunts and grandmother lived. "I
> see you're hanging out your sheets today," his Aunt
> Romayne would call from her back porch. "Yes," Bill's
> mother would shout back. "I thought the wind would
> dry them nice and fast."

Perhaps it was this rootedness that helped drive him inward, to the worlds of literature and music, and, as it seemed to me, give him permission to ignore many aspects of what I think of as the "real world." On the first day of our meeting up in Budapest, I wrote in my journal that it was great to see him, meet up, hear his stories, "but now he's become Philip Larkin, wishing he could visit China and go home the same afternoon."

My account of the ferry trip across the Tisza River goes like this. We had been taking lesser roads, much pleasanter, but we got confused when we tried to cross the river:

*My father managed several farms
for his grandfather in Hungary.*

Talk to man on bike. He says you have to find the *KOMP*. I pretend to understand, look up word, which means "ferry." His instructions excellent.

We arrive at top of steep bank, Tisza is at bottom. One car ahead of us. Woman in small outboard watching this side. Ferry delivering customers other side. Small crowd gathers. Eventually six cars, about 20 people, some on foot, get in ferry. Toothless, leathery Charon turns wheel. Younger, more ordinary fleshy fellow running the show. Have to remove one car to release ferry from bottom, then drive back on when loosened. Large passengers lend a hand. An adventure, makes me feel less a tourist.

Once across the river, we set out for the tiny village of Ecségfalva, where we stop at the ruins of a farm. Small railroad tracks emerge from what must have been a barn, and I remember that my father had written that his grandfather Jakabfy's farm, Cserepes, had had narrow-gauge rail tracks to carry the grain to Szolnok, where they switched to the wider gauge. Bill sits in our car while Will and I explore a bit. Is this the place? One of them? There were several farms. I am pleased, but uncertain. I take lots of pictures. Two years later, with my niece Katie, I will uncover more of the story with the help of a local schoolteacher and an

*In 1993 my niece Katie and I found two local
people who helped us locate those family sites.*

old farmer who had worked for my great-grandfather. Yes, this was one of the former family farms, and Katie and I will visit the sites of two others. I was continuing to make pilgrimages.

But it is on this visit with Bill that I visit my father's secondary school and talk with the director. The prestigious Evangélikus Gimnázium was known for producing math and science geniuses, including physicist Leo Szilard, Nobel physicist Eugene Wigner and John von Neumann, the brilliant mathematician who worked on the atomic bomb project. My father was not a genius, but he was a man of high intellect. I find his name on a wall in the school, a list of former students. In addition, Bill and I collect the last of the Hungarian money that my father had claimed after the war, based on ownership of property in Budapest he had inherited from his father. This involves a trip to a lawyer's office in the city. In a true bit of irony, the office is located in a building on the famous Andrássy Út—number 113—that once housed my family's apartment. We must spend the money in Hungary, and so it provides us with a free stay at the Gellért and a number of good meals.

At the end of our Hungarian visit, we travel westward, but not before spending an excruciating few hours in Budapest's Keleti Railroad Station, where I eventually manage to get tickets for Will's train to Paris and ours to Germany, France and Holland. This is in itself a somewhat fraught ride, overcrowded, with threats of losing our unreserved seats at various points. On the Hungarian border, the ticket taker demands an additional 2,000 forints, about $6 U.S. I note that "various German-speaking people and our small Hungarian (a worker who has been made to show his wallet) protest in vain about this surcharge, overcharge." Then we arrive in Munich, where Will leaves us to head for Paris. Here we find an entirely different sort of experience: a railroad station that is both pleasant and efficient, and with plenty of carts for our luggage. (There were, of course, none in Budapest.) We marvel at the ease of boarding as we depart for Strasbourg—no surcharge, no grumbling, clarity about reservations. The train is clean and comfortable, with plenty of room to stash luggage. We have brought bread, some oranges and drinks. The well-engineered railbed makes it possible to read and write, to peel an orange, hold a drink without spilling. Small children and old ladies can walk down the aisle with ease.

In Munich we stayed at the Arcade Hotel, which, as Bill remarked, "reminded us in no way of the Gellért. It was functional enough (what else was it?) and we headed out

in search of food." Meanwhile I have—typically—written
several pages in my notebook about the hotel, answering
his post-trip question about what else it was.

> The Arcade Hotel is full of Asian kids, squatting in
> the lobby, hanging about the alley next door, looking
> well-scrubbed, well-fed.
>
> The hotel fully functional, stripped-down, combi-
> nation monk's cell, hospital and boat interior. Every-
> thing from Habitat or Crate and Barrel, Conran's.
> All-white walls, bright blue tweed carpet, simplified
> fixtures—rod with hangers, grill racks, white enam-
> elled for clothes, ledge under window for sitting or
> suitcases. Room has handsome arched windows,
> Romanesque, aerodynamic. . . . Good buffet breakfast
> with waitresses who look like they hate jobs. People
> at reception like airline stewardesses. But it's sort of
> like a rest cure, at least momentarily—white, clean,
> comfortable.
>
> City big, prosperous, full of fashionable clothes
> (the first) and jewelry that makes me lustful for the
> first time on trip. Still, a little too self-congratulatory,
> grandiose, hot, crowded in main center—jammed
> with tourists. Two big museums handsome, especially
> Alte Pinakothek.

Here's Bill's take on the place after we'd walked around the first night, getting lost looking for a place to have a meal. He had been in Munich in 1951, when he traveled with the student band. They'd had a great time, but it was forty years later and the place had changed.

> My simple Munich, where you went to a café and ordered beer and sausage, wasn't immediately visible. It had been internationalized. Next morning, we walked in the already warming up morning to the Alte Pinakothek, which surely has claims to be the best museum visited during the two weeks. I managed to preserve seeing intensity for a longer period than sometimes. Afterwards we headed for early lunch and the requisite wurst (and beer) at an outdoor café. No longer living with Budapest [cheap] prices, and on our own money, there was a distinctly new hint to life. We located the Englischer Gardens but were too torpid to do much more than sit down, lie down by a little lake and watch the people cavorting. Further walking about the center of things and through the Hofbrau House, revealed a tourist Munich of some dimensions and showed us that the notion of a Pedestrian Mall isn't necessarily commensurate with a great place to walk.

We board another train, and after a full description of

this ride, my journal ends, except for brief notes about our time in Amsterdam. The train, however, gives me occasion to write—about the train:

> A respite between tourists'/travelers' responsibilities. The train is a cocoon. We're now à trois in a 6-person compartment. . . . Raining on and off. We missed the inside of Strasbourg Cathedral because huge crowds waited for the astronomical clock. Seemed too daunting. So bought long sandwiches and sat by the river? canal? for a few sunny moments . . . .
>
> Like other Euro-City trains, this one (named Iris) is clean, well-lit, comfortable. Conductor in Belgium discovers that we're routed wrong, should have changed in Lux., not Brussels. Elaborate calculations, comes up with $30 added to change of route. Says we can get money back where we bought it (in U.S.). I said I'd send him a postcard if we succeeded. His English excellent and he's proud of it. Spent time in U.S., Louisiana and Texas, mostly looking for records, a country-western fan. He complains that if the French tix-taker had done his job, we wouldn't have had to pay extra. A little chauvinism?

The "flourishing head cold" that Bill referred to at the start of his travel journal didn't appear until we got to

Amsterdam, then flourished fully and miserably during a drizzly trip to Haarlem. At the Rijksmuseum in Amsterdam, Bill noted:

> There were many recognizably American Tourists, that old type: men dutifully trying to respond to Dutch painting but looking as if they'd rather be having a coffee or beer somewhere. . . . Through my burgeoning cold I was able to summon up satisfaction in the area of Vermeer and Pieter de Hooch, but yearned for a more copious selection of Dutch Masters. Coming into Holland I had repeated the opening line to that Robert Lowell sonnet—"The cows of Potter and Albert Cuyp are timeless." In fact they were viewless. . . . The excuse was an upcoming Rembrandt show, but since that wasn't scheduled until December 1, the preparations seemed excessive.

This trip and our responses to it pointed out once again the sharp differences in our ways of traveling, in our temperaments and inclinations. Bill had cultivated a sort of not-always-ironic irritability, and his experience always found a literary track. There were, it's true, the pleasures of food, but more than anything, the validation, the consolation to be found in books.

We had a lovely pure dinner one evening, lamb-steak (and salmon) and the freshest vegetables and fine potatoes; and after Willy joined us, a splendid Indian one. In Amsterdam I felt, somehow even more strongly than in Budapest, Munich, Strasbourg, that I didn't know enough—didn't know much of anything and didn't bring the requisite equipment to the sights. But the great thing—maybe the greatest thing—about travel for me is the way it fuels the desire to read, different things, or reread old things, like Henry James's *Transatlantic Sketches.* So the experience is Wordsworthian after all—"the life and food for future years" spoken of in "Tintern Abbey."

It rained in Haarlem and Bill had a cold.

On the Road

By WILLIAM H. PRITCHARD

In a famous poem Robert Frost once gave us a picture of the road less traveled by, which is the one he took and which, he says, made all the difference. Everybody respects this poem, but as far as I can see nobody except me (and perhaps one or two others — I'd like to hear from them) puts into practice his advice, at least as far as driving a car from one place to another.

Take the relatively straightforward business of getting from Amherst, where I live, to Bradley Field, to which I sometimes have to drive departing relatives and guests. Only an hour, just get on Route 91 and let her rip. But what a boring hour, especially between the Ingleside mall area and Windsor Locks, always 90 degrees with all that humidity or else it's freezing rain and sleet. Lots of exhaust to smell. Nevertheless yesterday I forgot and drove that way in a hurry to get there. But coming back, with a twist of the imagination, I became an interesting person, a crank at the wheel who declined the dubious joys of 91 and opted instead for Route 75, Poquonock one way, Suffield the other. After circling Bradley Field and viewing the wrecked airplanes at what looks like a pretty wrecked air museum, you move on out into greenery, the cars become infrequent, and soon the gentle delights of Suffield, Conn. beckon to the musing traveler who by this time has felt free to muse. To the left and right are handsome houses, sloping lawns, a well-cared for private school, everything years away from the 91 straightaway or free-for-all.

For years now I've been turning into this imaginative, or crank, driver, particularly in the summertime when people have to be gotten here and there or parents have to be visited. Time was we drove to New York by using the Merritt Parkway, a pretty enough parkway, but suddenly one June I looked at a map and realized I could head over to Route 22 and drive right down to Westchester, passing through all manner of towns I'd never seen — Hillsdale and Amenia and Pawling. I made it, but at the cost of nearly breaking up our marriage, since it must have been 96 degrees that day and there were three small children my wife had to deal with in various parts of the car. A memorable experience, but not necessarily to be repeated. Coming back from Westchester recently, same wife but only one, quiet, child (it's 15 glorious years later), I avoided the gigantic Route 684 (which connects with 84 to zoom you all the way to Hartford) and drove up Route 100, a splendid old road which winds here and there through the upper reaches of Westchester, eventually merging with 202 and 6. At one point you can get on 84,

but do not continuing instead to drive along ancient Route 6 toward Connecticut. Suddenly you will look up and there on your right, a few yards from your elbow, you will see all the other drivers, whizzing along and trying to pass each other on 84. By this time your passengers have fallen asleep, and you will be there, all alone on ancient, obsolete 6, supremely happy.

Sometimes the most hateful or unlikeliest road may turn out by a stroke of fate to be the one you want. In the days before 91 and 84 you went from here to New York via Route 5, which south of Hartford turned into a horrible stretch called the Berlin Turnpike. In the 1950s there were scores of diners and garish eateries, with gas stations warring against each other (sometimes the stuff was going for 18 cents a gallon) and a series of traffic lights set for 40 miles per hour (or was it 45?) which one would ingeniously try to outwit and always fail. Then 91 was built, the gas stations and most of the eateries died, but the road is still there in all its vivid ugliness. Don't miss it next time down. And while you're at it, don't miss the Route 202 experience which you may hop onto in South Hadley or Westfield to end up in Maine or in Delaware. Or if you happen to be an Amherst resident on your way home from some point south, and if you've neglected to be imaginative and thus find yourself on 91 approaching Springfield, turn off immediately onto Route 21 which rather tediously negotiates Ludlow for awhile, but then marvelously opens out and turns into, surprisingly, Belchertown! This one takes a bit longer, but how much of a hurry are you in?

My mother believes in progress, prefers to drive on big highways, and after years of enduring Route 7 in New York State (Binghamton to Oneonta and endlessly beyond toward Albany, on the way to Massachusetts) I don't blame her. Now she has Route 88, an enormous, uncrowded, straight non-toll road with no "services" and no problems. When I'm ready to head back to Amherst from her place she always inquires which road I'm taking, and to relieve her mind, I say casually, "Oh 88 I guess, and she is pleased with my sensible judgment. Little does she know that almost as soon as I leave her house my crank-at-the-wheel personality takes over and before I can stop myself I am wandering over bumpy Route 23, through East Davenport and Prattsville and the obsolete Catskills.

It is good at such times to have as company the one person in my family who has, on occasion, not merely believed but approved and encouraged my behavior. Even he lost his patience one hot July afternoon on a drive home from the Adirondacks. I was contriving to avoid the thruway and turnpike, so managed to drive through Troy, N.Y., in order to head up exciting Route 2

between Troy and Williamstown, up and over the mountains. That part of it (after Troy) was fine, but somehow they'd rerouted things in Adams, and I ended up looking for Route 116 (always a good road to be on in its northwestern reaches) in a cornfield. The passenger instructed me to find the quickest road quick, and get us home. Which made me grateful that the time I got lost in Danbury, thank God nobody was along. What were you doing in Danbury?

Massachusetts residents can't be expected to care much about all the new state road lore I've get tucked away, so let me come home with some favorite byways and hot crank driving tips. If you have to go to New London, don't of course go 91, 2, and 11 (the fastest way) but wend your way leisurely to Belchertown and Palmer, where you pick up Route 32, move through cool forests, through Monson and Stafford Springs, no traffic, fine trip. Eventually there is Willimantic to be gotten through, but don't you owe it to yourself to see Willimantic once? When you get to New London, park your car and take the ferry to Long Island. Why not? And even though as big roads go, the Mass. Turnpike is

William Pritchard: discovering the longest distance between two points. (Photo by Gordon Daniels)

Another travel piece, this time about avoiding interstates—for our local paper.

Separate Accounts /
Parallel Lives

BEFORE BILL GAVE UP most forms of travel, there was a time when he did some traveling on his own, resulting in some writing, both published and not. On one occasion, in 1980, he wrote a piece for our local paper's weekend magazine, *Hampshire Life*, about his preference for driving on byways rather than highways. For that piece he designated himself as The Crank at the Wheel, noting that not all members of his family always enjoyed this sidewinding. Still, he persisted. "Sometimes," he wrote, "the most hateful or unlikeliest road may turn out by a stroke of fate to be the one you want." As an example he cites the Berlin Turnpike in Connecticut:

> In the days before the interstates 91 and 84, you went from here [Amherst] to New York via Route 5, which south of Hartford turned into a horrible stretch called the Berlin Turnpike. In the 1950s there were scores of diners and garish eateries, with gas stations warring against each other (sometimes the stuff was going for

18 cents a gallon) and a series of traffic lights set for
40 miles per hour, which one would ingeniously try
to outwit and always fail. Then 91 was built, the gas
stations and most of the eateries died, but the road is
still there in all its vivid ugliness. Don't miss it the
next time down. . . . Or if you happen to be an Amherst
resident on your way home from some point south,
and if you've neglected to be imaginative and thus
find yourself on 91 approaching Springfield, turn off
immediately onto Route 21, which rather tediously
negotiates Ludlow for awhile, but then marvelously
opens out into, surprisingly, Belchertown! This one
takes a little longer, but how much of a hurry are you in?

THE FOLLOWING YEAR, after a trip to Manhattan to see
the New York City Ballet and meet with some friends, he
wrote another account, reprising his designation, this time
titling his unpublished piece "A Crank in New York: or,
What Am I Doing in This Place?" With classic traveler's
postdeparture angst, he lists the things he has forgotten to
bring, none of them crucial, except for the opera glasses.
"I'd thought about them in the middle of the night, should
have gotten up right then and put them next to my
wallet. . . . I won't need them, anyway you spoil the sense
of the whole by focusing on one dancer." The toothbrush

and toothpaste, he notes, can be gotten at the drugstore around the corner from his hotel.

It is a hot day in the city and he has to calibrate his day, preserving the right kind of energy for different events— meeting friends for a substantial lunch, then getting ready to meet a friend for dinner at six before the evening performance. So after lunch, back to the hotel to cool off and have a nap, after which there are many decisions to be made:

> If you eat veal piccata at 1, plus liquid refresh and coffee, even a cigarette, what do you want at 6? The veal piccata is still very much there, and really we don't want to <u>walk</u> from here to Dimitri's do we? 22 blocks? As I remember the place is beyond Lincoln Center, must be in the mid sixties. Let's try the bus up 6th Ave., not so crowded. Whoops, oh, yes very crowded indeed. Still nobody gives up their seat anymore and the women standing in front of me look pretty healthy, don't seem pissed off that I haven't risen. But back in 4th grade we were told that a gentleman. . . . Those really were the days.

Once Bill had decided he was not going to leave home any more than necessary, I had to decide how I was going to continue to see more of the world than I could encompass on my daily walks with the dog. Starting in 1988, we had regularly spent a summer week in Westport on the Massachusetts coast. That continued until 2010, when Bill was recovering from a bout of depression that seemingly came out of the blue, lasted for more than a year, then went back to wherever it had come from. Bad weather for most of that week-long stay combined with Bill's dark mood persuaded us to end what had been a happy vacation arrangement of twenty-plus years. But Westport wasn't exactly travel. We spent most of our time reading on the deck or in the yard looking out at the river, with short forays for grocery shopping, swimming (me), walks on the beach (both of us) and some socializing with a few people we knew in the town. That routine wasn't replaced with any sort of firm vacation plans. We began, instead, doing some shorter road trips to visit friends and relations during the long academic summer. At other times during the year Bill would still go to places where he had been asked to speak on a literary subject or attend a memorial for a literary figure, so we went together to Cincinnati for an Updike conference, to New York for Anthony Hecht's memorial service and to Baltimore, where Bill gave a talk at Johns Hopkins. But there were no more long flights on planes for him—his chronic back problem—

2001: Bill with John Updike at a conference in Cincinnati.

and besides, he was content with his books, his music, his teaching.

I was not ready to join him in his geriatric routine. So we had to work something out. Even before his retreat into the familiar, I had done some traveling, solo or with others. I made—and continue to make—those twice yearly trips to Oregon. Bill made those trips with me a few times, but stopped when seven hours on a plane was too much for his back. But starting in the '70s I had ventured out on my own—first to see friends on the West Coast, then, beginning in 1989, to explore places in Central Europe connected to my family. In September of 2005 my sister and I took part in a Country Walkers walking tour in Sicily, the first—and until now, the last—group trip I've been on. My travel journal now had a double goal—keeping track of impressions for myself, as before, but now also for Bill. He would often keep a parallel journal at home to let me know what he'd been up to in my absence. As always, his pages were amusing, literate, literary, sometimes gossipy, and often focused on his small-scale adventures with the dog and with preparing meals. I had arranged to write a story about my sisterly Sicilian trip for the local paper, and so I kept a journal that was more detailed than usual. The eventual article was much less personal than what, in an unusual move, I typed

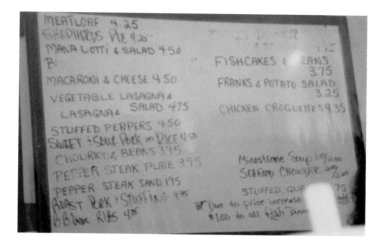

A favorite restaurant's menu in Little Compton, Rhode Island,
near where we rented a place in Westport, Massachusetts.

up for Bill and myself, and have excerpted here.

The army always, in both of our accountings, marches firmly on its stomach. Both of us in our journals record our meals, knowing that the other will be interested, appalled or amused. Here are some parts from our notes to ourselves and each other that we wrote in the summer of 2005, starting with mine:

Wed., Sept. 21, 2005

I fill up the morning at home with small chores, walk the dog uptown to return extra books on Sicily to the public library, water the yellow begonia under Mother and Daddy's niche in the columbarium.

On my way out of the driveway to pick up Bill after his class to take me to the airport, I hear a crunch. I have backed up over one of my favorite plants, a pottted ivy geranium. Bad luck. If I were a Sicilian, this might spoil my trip. In front of Converse where Bill has his class, I immediately find a place to park. Good luck.

I spend the night in Alexandria, Virginia, with my sister. In the early 1980s, Dodo and I had several times hiked in the White Mountains, staying in the Appalachian Mountain Club's huts for a few nights. We both liked to walk, and after our mother's death in 2003, we decided to devote some of our modest inheritance to doing some traveling together. She would have approved, we thought. And so we signed up for this walking tour. Dodo's husband, Charley, drives us to Dulles airport, where my journal continues.

We mill around in an un-airconditioned section until, without any announcement, Alitalia begins putting people on a vehicle to take us to the plane. Chaos and confusion reign when a woman in a wheelchair cannot be transferred from the vehicle to the plane.

Then we sit on the tarmac for 1½ hours. The only explanation from the pilot is that we don't yet have a "flight plan." Still, dinner arrives shortly after we depart. Prosciutto with green beans, a beef pot-roast thing (Dodo has pasta with ricotta), a good roll, some fruit. When asked, the rather surly crew provides wine. Surliness is definitely the order of the day, a mode that I remember from previous Alitalia flights. Passengers are treated like slightly annoying intrusions into what could otherwise be a relaxing flight for the employees. . . .

The Milan airport, new to me, is both flashier (fancy shops) and grubbier (toilets) than expected. Still, Dodo has a nice-looking croissant. I mostly seem to want juice. They squeeze the oranges, and I have my first wonderful *spremuta di arancia*.

Both crew and plane on the way to Catania are pleasanter than the trans-Atlantic equivalents. We see some rocky islands in the sea—our destination for later?—and a top-down view of Etna, sprawled out amazingly. Big, big, black momma. At Catania, we wait for our luggage in the regular place, then learn that all coming from the U.S. must go to a separate room for screening. There are dogs, metal detectors. We are the most dangerous people in the world.

Meanwhile, Bill is describing my departure and his first couple of days on his own:

Wednesday, Sept. 21, 2005

Lovely day and we both woke up not too sleepless and walked up to the chapel. I taught *Secret Agent* (big scene) and then toiled over "Three Years She Grew" with the freshmen. Then M. picked me up with Kirby [our corgi] and a sandwich, drove to Bradley, said goodbye. Kirby and I had a v. smooth trip back.

The idea is to Pay Attention these ten days, try to enjoy oneself, get a lot of reading and preparation done, and don't have indigestion. In bed by eleven, no excesses of drink allowed.

I received cover for the Updike book [his book on the author, to be published in October]. . . .

That night, after I fried up the pork some more and watched the Red Sox disastrously lose, I prepared K. for bed and in process of getting up as well as picking out her water dish, I stumbled against the crate, scaring the shit out of her. She went to middle of kitchen, stood there without moving. No "go to your room" [command for going into her crate for the night]. So I headed upstairs, and so did she, settling in on the futon, where she stayed quietly all night until we got up!

Thursday:

Determined not to startle Kirby today. But she star-
tled me in the afternoon when, walking with Jeanne
Leinhardt [a former student], Kirby suddenly darted
beneath a shrub and emerged holding a chipmunk.
I was shocked, yelled Drop It, sort of pulled it away
from her. She didn't give it up willingly, on the other
hand she didn't bite into it, for the chipmunk, who
stood paralyzed for a spell, then disappeared. Shaken,
we continued our walk!

Ham steak and polenta for supper, good dependable
food. No Red Sox, so almost finished the [Jim] Guetti
memoir, also reading *Some Do Not* for class tomorrow.

As all this is happening, my sister and I have installed ourselves at the Grand Hotel Siracusa, which is, as I note,
"grand indeed," with strawberry-blond wood and marble
everywhere, Venetian glass fixtures. We have arrived a
couple of days before the tour starts, to get our bearings
and get over our jet lag.

The jacuzzi in our room is not to be fathomed, so
we use the shower. Dodo immediately wonders if we
have enough of a view. Hotel has promised, she says,

that every room has a view. We can see the sea, but
not enough for her taste. . . .

Ortygia, the island where we are staying, is the old,
nicely restored part of Siracusa. The real city is on the
mainland, not a haven for tourists. We take a walk on
the sunny seaside corso below the Piazza del Duomo,
then have a meal of antipasti and gelati at a restaurant
looking at the water and offering a "menu turistico."
Very satisfying. Then home for a nap. . . .

Tour minus 1: Saturday, Sept. 24

Not knowing that breakfast is "incluso" with our
room, we go out to find it. It's a pretty spot one level
up over the bay. I have a great *spremuto di arancia* along
with a somewhat heavy but extremely satisfying pas-
try/ham/cheese combination. My Italian is turning
out to be serviceable, if ungrammatical. I can hear
the difference in the Sicilian speech, but can mostly
make out what's said to me—meaning, I guess, they
speak Italian rather than the other dialect/language.
(But why is "Dalla Sua Pace" from *Don Giovanni* going
through my head all the time?)

In Amherst, Bill is enjoying a brilliant, cool, sunny day,
with his usual attention on the dog.

My sister, Dodo, and I on Mount Etna on a walking tour of Sicily in September 2005.

Kirby bounded out of room [crate] and kept up lively spirits with some excellent romping on the playing fields. No chipmunk in sight. I started up my Ogden Nash review, read freshmen papers. Joey DeMott called with news of Ben, which I passed on to a few. [Ben DeMott was recovering from heart surgery.] This was the first ring of the phone, followed by another, a hopeful tennis player who forgot "she was in Sicily." I successfully cleaned off my defective (smudged) Elgar CD with the cloth Julie [English department administrative assistant] so thoughtfully provided. These little triumphs are not to be sneezed at. The Red Sox won again, tying things up with Yankees.

In Sicily, the tour is beginning, and at breakfast on the rooftop of the Grand Hotel, we encounter one of our tour companions, Mary Jane Edwards, the daughter of Toni Lukacs, who was once a suitor of our mother's back in Budapest and Vienna.

She is small, compact, fast-talking and mother-henny, simultaneously deferring to and bossing her tall, stolid, wryly amusing and often amused scientist husband. They both turn out to be witty and good company. Mary Jane is avidly curious about things,

wanting always, for instance, to have the Latin names
for plants. . . .

Dodo and I walk around the main city center. The
Piazza del Duomo is a handsome open, oval space
slightly tilted away from the baroque cathedral where
people sit out to eat and drink and watch. Italians
know how to construct public places. . . . A museum
we want to get into is *chiuso* for repairs. I flash back on
our previous life in Italy when things would always be
closed for one reason or another. *Oggi festa* [today is
a holiday], seemingly a random event, is my favorite.

We gather in the hotel lobby to have our first group
meeting. There are ten of us plus two guides. Several of
the people have been on a number of these tours before
and are wearing a lot of Country Walker gear—hats,
T-shirts, etc.; a couple of our companions have never been
out of the U.S. before.

We get onto our bus for the first time—a full-sized
vehicle with room for 40—and meet our driver, Malio,
a rotund man, moon-faced, slightly simian with
a small beard, who will become Malio the Great as
we learn to admire his driving skills and imperturb-
ability on the high, winding, narrow switchbacks we

will later encounter. As for his appearance, Dodo says that their friend Justice Scalia has said to expect to see a lot of people in Sicily who look like him. This seems especially true of the men. The women are more elegant, hawk-nosed, ferocious.

THE TOUR DEVELOPS A ROUTINE. The first day there is less walking and more looking as we visit an archeological park filled with ancient monuments from various periods. Sicily, perhaps even more than some parts of the Mediterranean, was inhabited and conquered by many different peoples—the Greeks, the Romans, the Arabs among them. As I note, "We spend too much time in the catacombs hearing the story of how our guide and a tourist couple almost got locked in there. Not encouraging." We go home to nap, shower, change and get ready for the first of many communal and banquet-like meals. This one involves "a many-layered, complex antipasto: spinach, eggplant, omelet with ricotta, caponata, etc.; then three pastas, followed by three fishes, a torrone and the possibility of freshly filled cannoli." One of our number is enlisted to try his hand at filling a few cannolis, to much cheering. A version of this meal—with three choices for each course, except for the antipasto, which is more like

I found shade from the fierce Sicilian
sun in a Romanesque cloister.

a dozen—will be repeated many times. We get used to eating late—8:30–9—and getting up early.

AS WE TRAVEL BY BUS and on foot together, our group begins to coalesce. We learn about each others' lives, backgrounds and food preferences. Running jokes develop. One of our number, Big Charlie (there are two Charlies of different sizes, who are friends), likes to ask our guide teasingly specific numerical questions. When we visit a volcano on the island of Vulcano, we learn that it is older than Etna. "How old?" Big C asks. Instead of throwing up his hands, Sebastiano teases back: Exactly 857,436 years. Big C is a joker, but I learn that he, like several others in the group, is here to iron out his soul. He is a top executive at Marsh & McLennan, a huge New York insurance and management consulting firm, an unembarrassedly rich man. His offices were in one of the twin towers that were destroyed on 9/11/01, and though he wasn't there that day, he knew and had hired most of the more than three hundred M&M employees who were killed in the attack. Little C says Big C went to all of those funerals, called up all of those families, and four years later is still recovering.

As is true of most travels, I've found, the impressions that come to us are usually more vivid and memorable than those we experience in daily life. Travel is not just broadening, as the old claim would have it, but it's focusing. It's like some moments in sport—tennis is mine—when you can see the ball more clearly, and it even seems to slow up as it comes toward you. No wonder I have so much more to say from Sicily than Bill has from home. I am taking nothing for granted, have no habits to carry me toward a comfortable routine and possible boredom.

But Bill is not bored. He is fully engaged with his daily rounds, and especially with the wide range of reading he does. I am always amazed, impressed, when I read his writing (I am his first editor) at how much he knows and continues to absorb. When he reviews a book he will read not only that book, but go back and read or reread the author's other works. If it is a biography, he will read or reread other biographies of the same person. He carries all this lightly, unpedantically. It is what he loves to do; it is his life.

He is equally engaged with the small events of his life, with a range that gets smaller as the years go by. His trips to the library are adventures, as his knees and back become less reliable. Most of the books he wants—literary ones— are on C level, three stories below the entrance. He doesn't take the stairs anymore, but uses the elevator. Still it is a challenge. The stacks on that level are the frightening moveable sort, created to make it possible to cram more books into a smaller footprint. You press a button and the shelves move aside, creating an aisle that you walk into, imagining always that horror-movie scenario where you are crushed by the shelves as they close on their own or by some unseen malevolent hand. As you step in, the pressure of your foot keeps the stacks open and turns lights on—or is supposed to. None of this ever works perfectly, and in addition, by Bill's account, the books he wants are almost always on the bottom shelf, just off the floor, leaving him wondering whether he will be able to get up after retrieving them on his knees.

Trips to the supermarket or a doctor's appointment in Northampton are likewise sources of rich anecdotes. A traffic jam, a thunderstorm, a chance meeting with an old acquaintance or the absence of enough checkout lanes occupy his imagination. He is delighted or appalled by the antics of our dog. He watches and keeps up with the Red Sox and especially the Celtics, watches some old movies but few recent ones. He has e-mail contact with a few friends, "regular" letters from a few others, to his great pleasure, and we have some social contact with another few. Daniel Mendelsohn, in a nice piece of writing in *The New Yorker*, describes a cruise he took with his eighty-one-year-old father that retraced the journey of Odysseus through the Mediterranean. The son had taught a college course about the *Odyssey*, and the father had sat in on it. The father is smart and cranky, prickly both in the classroom and out, but on the trip he relaxes and charms his son as well as the other passengers. Earlier, when they were reading the book, the father had complained about the so-called hero of the piece, drawing up what the son refers to as "an extended charge sheet of Odysseus' failings. 'He's a liar and he cheated on his wife.'. . . 'He's always crying.'. . . 'What's so *haihroic* about that?' " Besides, argues the father, "Everything he does, every bit of success he has, is really because the gods help him." On the trip, they visit many of the sites named in the poem, and the father begins to repeat his conviction that "the poem feels more real." In the end, because of worker strikes all over Greece, they are not able to reach Ithaki, the island where Odysseus's journey began and ended. The captain, in a shrewd move, asks Mendelsohn to read aloud to the passengers the Greek poet Constantine Cavafy's "Ithaca." This is a poem,

Mendelsohn writes, "about the virtues of not arriving."
He likes the idea, he tells his father, that "we've kept the
ending at bay. The story can go on and on."

The father's response reminds me a little of my husband,
choosing art over life:

> After a pause, he said, 'So I was right all along.' His
> voice was sly; the sombre mood had evaporated. "Right
> about what?"
>   "The poem actually is more real than the place!"

Bill and our corgi, Ripley, share space in our house.

Wedding, August 1957, and fifty years later.

The Long Journey

Speech after long silence; it is right,
All other lovers being estranged or dead,
Unfriendly lamplight hid under its shade,
The curtains drawn upon unfriendly night,
That we descant and yet again descant
Upon the supreme theme of Art and Song:
Bodily decrepitude is wisdom; young
We loved each other and were ignorant.

—W. B. Yeats

WRITERS HAVE OFTEN compared life to a journey. We start here and we end up there. That word—"journey"—began by meaning a day's travel, the French *une journée,* from the Latin *diurnus.* I enjoy these etymologies and these bits of verbal trivia, which is lucky, since I've often had jobs as an editor, and my curiosity about words keeps the work from being drudgery. A dictionary sits on the windowsill in the kitchen where Bill and I do most of our eating, and an online dictionary is bookmarked on my computer.

A journeyman, I learn, was originally one who worked by the day. Journey: We've lost the sense of time that word once implied, but we've kept the travel part. So maybe life is a journey, or is it a trip? Hardly anyone has compared life to a trip, unless they meant it in the old hippie definition of being high on drugs—tripping. "Journey" feels more dignified, more significant, somehow. But what about "travel"? That word's history suggests a whole other side of things. It began by meaning suffering, painful labor, as in childbirth—*travail*. The word remains in French simply as "work."

Bill and I have been traveling, sometimes travailing, together as husband and wife for sixty years as of August 2017. It has been quite a journey, even quite a trip at times. There are many moments to remember and some others that are better forgotten. This little book, an account of our travels and nontravels, takes in only one aspect of our relationship, mostly leaving out extended accounts of our professional lives, our lives as the parents of three sons, our friendships, our connections to extended family, our everyday struggles and routines. It leaves out the love affair that brought us together, the conflicts that have threatened but not broken our bond. Travel is the exception to ordinary life, the exception, you might say, that proves the rule. It shines a spotlight on our characters during the relatively short time span before we return to "ordinary" life. It's a kind of test that sometimes pits us one against the other. Sometimes we have done better at it, sometimes not so well.

As I have noted earlier, Bill and I have never been major risk takers in our travels. Our forays into the unknown have always had a strong element of the known. But even when you think you know what to expect, have prepared yourself with guidebooks and language study, there will be surprises, just as in the rest of life.

BILL AND I are both in our ninth decade, and many of those decades have been spent in each other's company. These numbers are just numbers, but they also mean something in terms of losses, if not gains. Have we begun in delight and ended in something like wisdom, as Robert Frost said a poem should do? Have we gained any wisdom through the years? Or, is it simply, as Yeats wrote, that "Bodily decrepitude is wisdom"?

Here are the lyrics of a wonderful Billie Holiday song. They beautifully exemplify a cliché beloved of children's and other writers: the bluebird of happiness can be found right in your own backyard. Oh, sure, the ambitious traveler replies. What about the pyramids? The Parthenon? Angkor Wat? But of course, as a wise friend once pointed out, clichés are clichés for a good reason: They work. For most of us, our backyard is about as far as we'll be traveling at the very end of things. So why not find whatever happiness might be waiting there?

The bird with feathers of blue, is waiting for you,
Back in your own back yard,
You'll see your castle in Spain, through your window pane,
Back in your own back yard.
Oh you can go to the East, go to the West,
But someday you'll come weary at heart
Back where you started from.
You'll find your happiness lies, right under your eyes,
Back In Your Own Backyard.

Back in our own backyard.

ACKNOWLEDGMENTS

WITHOUT BILL'S WILLINGNESS to share his journals and recollections, this little book would not have been possible.

My gratitude, as in the past, goes to the meticulous and graceful work of designer James McDonald and to the meticulous and unsparing editing of Chris Jerome.

The photo opposite, taken in 2014, shows Bill and me with all of our children and grandchildren. Standing, from left, Mike and Will; seated on steps, David, Avery, George and David, with Ripley the corgi.

May all their journeys be illuminating, rewarding and worth the travail.